Alberto De Luigi

Justice as Equality and Neutrality

createspace^{tm}

ISBN-10: 1508995230
ISBN-13: 978-1508995234

Printed by CreateSpace
Charleston (SC)
March 2015

Abstract

The ideal of liberal neutrality and the ideal of equality are often seen as a trade-off. If the State has to be neutral between the interests of the rich and the poor, it is supposed to not intervene redistributing resources between them. Neutrality is thus associated to the ideal of a laissez-faire free market system, while equality is generally seen as an ideal requiring State policies aiming at equal opportunity. In this book neutrality and equality are presented as compatible and complementary ideals, rather than antagonist. First, it is shown that the moral justification of neutrality ultimately relies on a particular ideal of equality called "equal respect". Second, there are principles of justice and State policies aimed at improving equality of opportunity that can be neutrally justifiable. It is also provided a neutral justification of Rawls' difference principle, showing even how libertarian thinkers may agree on it.

The Author

Alberto De Luigi (Ponte dell'Olio, 1990) studied at the University of Milan and achieved a Bachelor degree in Political Science and a Master degree in Economics. He has always been passionate about political philosophy. He is one of three founding members of the cultural association Lodi Liberale, inaugurated in November 2013. In August 2014 he became Local Coordinator of the South European area for the international association Students for Liberty.

i

Table of Contents

Introduction

Justice can be defined as the right order of human relationships, but what it does in essence mean depends on the moral rules we assume as required by justice. This essay investigates the moral foundations of justice and finds its fundamental pillar in the principle of equal respect[1] (§2.2), a principle concerning equality among persons. Equal respect is not respect towards beliefs, rather towards persons. Some beliefs deserve our respect, others not, while equal respect requires us to recognize the capacity, that everyone possesses, for working out a coherent view of the world. When we face disagreement in discussing about the political rules we have to adopt, equal respect demands that we start a "rational dialogue" (§2.1) with our counterparts (rather than prevail by physical force, for instance). In fact, if a person shows her willingness to discuss rationally with us, then we have the moral *obligation* to discuss rationally with her. It will be explained why equal respect can be considered a moral principle shared by all in the western world, with few exceptions and limits. The term "equality" in the title *Justice as Equality and Neutrality* refers precisely to the notion of equal respect.

While equal respect is a moral ideal, the principle of rational dialogue is instead purely procedural: in order to be practiced it is not necessary to rely on a specific conception of the good life[2].

---

[1] Larmore [1987, 59]

[2] The notion refers to John Ralws' comprehensive conception:

"A conception is said to be general when it applies to a wide range of subjects (in the limit to all subjects); it is comprehensive when it includes conceptions of what is of value in human life, as well as ideals of personal virtue and character, that are to inform much of our non-political conduct (in the limit our life as a whole). There is a tendency for religious and philosophical conceptions to be general and fully comprehensive; indeed. Their being so is sometimes regarded as an ideal to be realized"

John Rawls [1993, V, §1, 175]

1

Rational dialogue is "neutral" with respect to all the controversial conceptions of the good life present in the society. In fact when we face disagreement it requires that we try to convince the other part on the basis of her own beliefs. If not even in this case we agree on a solution, we have to leave aside our personal convictions in order to reach an agreement about a more general aspect of the problem, establishing a procedure that doesn't rely on particular controversial conceptions of the good, or interests of the parts involved (the simplest example of neutral procedure is to put the matter to the vote). Since equal respect represents the moral justification of rational dialogue, the concept of neutrality is not to be opposed, but considered as complementary to equality. Rational dialogue also applies to political decisions when taken by a ruler, then "neutrality" means that political authority has not the purpose nor the right to promote a value or another kind of affiliation to a particular controversial conception of the good life. This is the theory of "political liberalism", a conception of liberal State based on the principle of neutrality. The second chapter is devoted to explain all these themes at length and represents the conceptual core of the essay. In order to fully understand the moral validity of this theory of justice, it is necessary to deal with an important premise, treated in the first chapter.

Equal respect is a moral requirement with *normative* implications, but it relies on a *factual* condition: pluralism (§1.6). In a nutshell, pluralism means that the more we talk, the more we disagree, even when dealing with persons we consider reasonable[3]. Pluralism is not intended as a doctrine here, rather as a "state of affairs" of political world: it doesn't require a relativistic perspective nor demand we promote or afford a plurality of

---

[3] For the time being, with the term "reasonable" we generically indicate persons willing "to propose and abide by fair terms of social cooperation among equals" (Rawls [1993, III, §1.2, 94]). In paragraph 2.2 the concept of reasonableness will be explained in deep.

values we shall consider "equally objective"[4], rather it simply consists in accepting that citizens of present western societies embrace many different values they will never agree about. To explain this, both analytical and historical reasoning are provided. The first chapter faces this challenge, starting from the historical origin of the word *neutrality* and its concept (§1.1), investigating its relations with the idea of tolerance (§1.2, §1.3), pluralism and modernity (§1.6, §1.7). It may appear odd, but the most powerful justification of pluralism is given by our own inner moral conflicts, rather than by conflicts with other persons. In fact there are two different and conflicting "patterns" of moral reasoning that appear to have both equally moral validity to ourselves: deontology and consequentialism (§1.7). Since morality has heterogeneous patterns and in certain cases we cannot even redeem ourselves from these conflicts, to reach an agreement with others is by far a more intricate task, often impossible.

All these topics covered in the first two chapters owe much to Charles Larmore's theory of political liberalism. Rawls' theory of justice as fairness fits well with the theoretical framework of Larmore's political liberalism (§2.3). Nevertheless, Larmore also moves criticism against the "ambiguity" present in *A Theory of Justice* (1971); criticism that is acknowledged by Rawls, as he admits in *Political liberalism* (1993) (§2.3). The third chapter does not deal only with the debate between the two philosophers, it even provides an answer to the question Larmore leaves unanswered: can Rawls' difference principle be justified under a liberal perspective? This principle only permits inequalities on condition that they work to the advantage of the worst off in society. At a first glance, the principle may look too controversial to be legitimate: the idea that society has to distribute "primary goods" in order to maximize the condition of the poorest hardly seems neutral between the interests of the rich and the poor,

---

[4] See Berlin [1991, 79-80].

while a principle of justice should necessarily maintain itself neutral in order to reach a liberal justification. From this point of view, it could seem that there is a trade-off between the concepts of neutrality and equality: equality policies are often considered as non-neutral State intervention, while laissez-faire would closer resemble a neutral approach to redistributive issues. Despite appearances, after having provided a long analysis of the principle, it would be presented a neutral justification to it.

The principle of difference states that inequalities are to be arranged so that they benefit the worst off in society. But inequalities have to benefit the worst off in the long run, not (at least not necessarily) in the short period (§3.2). It doesn't exclude that an anarcho-capitalist system may improve the condition of the poorest more than a welfarist system inclined to State aid policies, maybe thanks to economic efficiency and a greater growth of production. It is often an empirical claim regarding economics (§3.6, §4.4), not a divergence on moral arguments, which divides liberists[5] from left liberals. The worst off individual is considered "worst off" for what regards the distribution of particular resources, that are the primary goods (§3.3). It's not a matter of allocation of wealth or welfare, like the maximin principle entails. The maximin principle raises a completely different issue from the difference principle, despite what many authors thought (§3.1). Primary goods are measured in a complex index, which includes, besides wealth or income, even liberties and the basis of self-respect, among which there is the right on property, as Rawls himself states (§3.5). It means that if primary goods as liberties and private property are at risk, and if they are considered of utmost importance in order to define who is actually the "worst off" in society, in the sense that who is deprived of her property is considered the one in the worst condition, then redistribution of wealth or other primary goods might be denied. In this case libertarians might accept the

---

[5] Laissez-faire supporters.

difference principle, which would simply represent a justification for economic inequalities without redressing them (§3.6).

There are other policies aiming at equal opportunity that may be justified from a neutral perspective, including a particular kind of inheritance tax (§4.1) and an insurance against bad luck (§2.7). In the economic world, the moral requirements of equal respect are compatible with the conception of "equality of resources"[6], to a large extent matching with the procedures of free market (§2.7); the conception of "equality of welfare" is instead rejected (§2.6).

Important criticisms to political liberalism are moved from communitarians and libertarians. The communitarian critique is partially rejected and counterarguments are presented, though it grasps some crucial points revealing the authentic limits of the principle of equal respect. These topics are handled in the second chapter (§2.4, §2.5). The fourth chapter is entirely addressed to libertarians. It does not represent an apology of the left-wing liberalism (even called "high liberalism") against libertarianism. On the contrary, it is a genuine incitement to thinkers who consider themselves libertarian to cultivate their economic theories, that are actually interesting and stimulating, dropping the claim to justify them by the traditional dogmatic beliefs belonging to the libertarian doctrine. It will be shown that the moral foundations of libertarianism represent a very controversial conception of the good life not universally valid nor sharable. Despite this, among the widespread libertarian economic tradition, there are theories that can be readapted in a completely different moral framework enjoying so a new light. Libertarian economic theories can be useful to test the efficacy of institutions or to discover their harmful aspects, to improve the efficiency of regulatory norms and, ultimately, to implement the conditions required by the difference principle.

Here it follows a graphical representation of the main concepts developed in the essay. Some notions in the graph are not

---

[6] Dworkin [2000].

mentioned in the introduction offered above. Topics of the same chapter have the same borderline graphic.

Figure 1: Justice as Equality and Neutrality

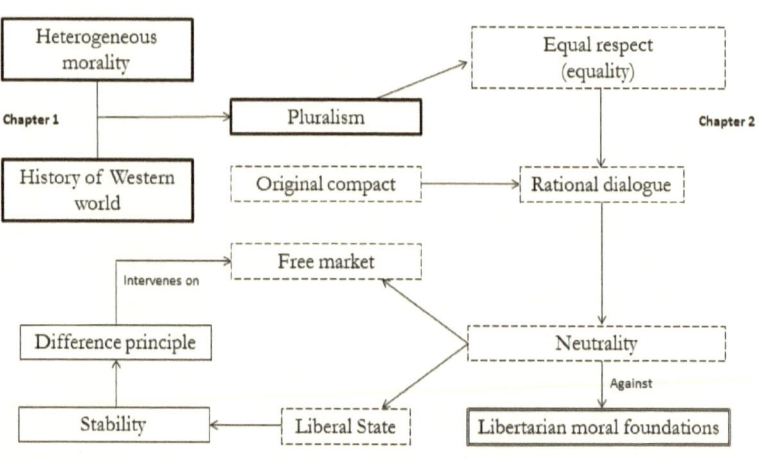

1.   Neutrality

1.1   Introduction to the Concept

Neutrality can be defined as the attitude to abstain from taking sides in a conflict, in favour of one or the other contender. It is a term commonly used with regard to international relationships, and abstention is intended as related to the intervention in an international conflict between States. But the concept is not limited to this framework. The fact of taking sides in favour of one of the contenders can be understood in very general terms, such as a military, economic or cultural advantage, while contenders in the conflict can be of the most varied nature: national states, political parties, social groups, individuals, and so on. Every journalist or historian should deal with neutrality in describing recent events taking place nearby. In public spaces passionate cultural or political debates are held between two or more views of reality, or ideologies, that try to counter each other, then the journalist shall refrain from siding one or another "faction" in order to be neutral. But this requirement is generally ascribable to a mere matter of objectivity, rather than neutrality. For the historian to be objective is a concern required by the discipline of history in order to properly carry out her work, while the issue of neutrality rises only when to provide a particular outlook implies to give an actual advantage to one particular side (for instance in terms of popular consensus). Therefore distinctions between neutrality and other concepts, like objectivity, are needed to avoid misunderstandings. Alan Montefiore has developed an accurate semantic analysis of the concept[7], underlining some essential elements of neutrality. First

---

[7] In *Neutrality and Impartiality: The University and Political Commitment* [1975]

7

of all, to be neutral means to be neutral between two or more actual or potential policies, or parties. Without the existence of disagreement, neutrality is not possible and the neutral part shall be in the position to exert some influence, having actual opportunity to choose whether to exercise it or not. The neutral part is not necessarily a "third" party with respect to a conflict: if it happens, it results in a particular case of neutrality, where at least one of the contenders abstracts from her own interests. This does not imply that the neutral part is indifferent to future developments of the situation, since *indifference* is a concept neutrality shall be distinguished from. To be indifferent means to have no preferences for a state of affairs or another. This is in turn different from *disinterest* and *detachment*. To be disinterested means to have no interests in the state of affairs, at least not consciously. It is close to but distinct from indifference, since having no preferences for a party or another does not necessarily mean having no interest in the fact of elections: for example they can be considered both good or bad, or both equally distant from a third party that is the one preferred. On the other hand detachment may be intended as setting aside whatever personal preferences one may happen to have. It is compatible with indifference, but does not presupposes it. Neutrality does not necessarily presupposes indifference and disinterest towards the results of a conflict, but if the neutral part happen to have certain preferences, it shall consider the matter at issue in an entirely detached spirit, abstracting from personal preferences.

It is interesting to note how the concept of neutrality changed over time until to reach the liberal connotation. In ancient times, the concept can be found in famous expression from Latin and Greek world, as well as in the Old Testament. The most renowned example is in Thucydides' *Peloponnesian War*, report of the conflict between Athens and Sparta for the control over Greece and Aegean sea (431-404 b.C.). The episode is the dialogue between Melians and Athenians, held between the inhabitants of Melos island, an indipendent Spartan colony that remained *neutral* in the conflict, and the στρατηγοί (*strategoi*) of Athens pretending their submission (the isle didn't bow and was conquered in 416 b.C). Though Melians' conduct can be correctly regarded as an example of neutrality, in the sense of abstention from a military conflict, a specific term to define the concept is not used yet. In Thucydides' sentences appeared the terms μηδ-έτερος[8] (composed of μηδέ and έτερος), which means "neither of them", or ουδετερος[9], which literally means "neuter" (the grammatical gender). As the Greek language, ancient Latin does not present a specific term, since it is used *neuter* either for the grammatical gender and for the abstention from conflicts. In this last case it is combined with the term *pars*, as in the expressions from Cicero *homo neutris partis* (neutral man), *neutram in partem effici possunt* (neither to harm nor benefit) or *neutram in partem moveri* (be indifferent). Instead the word *neutralis* (Quintilian) is only referred to the grammatical gender neuter[10]. In the sphere of politics the word *neutralitas* appears first in Latin literature in the XV century: the older instance is to be found in Nicholas of Cusa[11], reporting the events of the conflict between Pope Eugene IV and the council Fathers of Basel. When the Pope decided to move the Concilium to Ferrara (1438), the Fathers elected Antipope Felix V, provoking a schism which ended in 1449, with the spontaneous resignation of Felix. During the schism, the prince-electors of Roman Holy Empire declared themselves *neutral* between the Pope and the Fathers. Since then, the term is increasingly widespread, as it can be seen in numerous manuscripts from the collection of Sir

---

[8] Declined in μηδετεροις [Thucydides, 2007, 5.98].

[9] Declined in ουδετερων, [Thucydides, 2007, 5.84].

[10] See Luigi Castiglioni and Scevola Mariotti [2007], Karl Ernst Georges [2002].

[11] *Quod recedere de neutralitate seu ultralitate sit necessarium* (ca. 1442). See Nicholas of Cusa [2007].

Thomas Phillips[12], dating back to the Thirty Years War, in particular with reference to the neutral position of Sweden (which participates actively in the conflict only in 1630). In vernacular language it was even more common: in XVI century the term *neutralità* appears in numerous Machiavelli's passages with regard to politics[13], while other authors like Pietro Bembo[14] used it with reference to gender distinctions. According to Treccani encyclopedia [1997] the word *neutrale* was appearing in France, in Italy, in Germany, by the end of the XV to the XVII century, and was recorded by Wolff in his *Jus Gentium* (1749) as common term used in vernacular language to indicate those Grotius called *medii in bello (dicuntur vulgo neutrales)*[15]. Until this moment in time the concept of neutrality was always referred to

---

[12] Sir Thomas Phillips' collection of 49 manuscripts about the history of Thirty Years War (Liège, ca. 1635), in Latin, French and Italian: *Sacra Regia Maiestas Sueciae, perspecto Ducis Bavariae, et Catholicae Ligae obtinendas Neutralitatis desiderio...; Copia litterarum Capituli Trevirensis ad Imperatorem ob Neutralitatem ab Electore cum Sueco initam; Copia epistolae Capituli Trevirensis ad suum Electorem, circa Neutralitatem cum Rege Sueciae initam* (Trier, 16 February 1632); *Copia de inita ab Electore Trevirensis cum Rege Sueciae Neutralitate, protectioneque Francorum* (Ehrenbreitstein, 20 January 1632).
See http://www.zvab.com/angebote/louis-roy.html

[13] See for example *The Prince* (1532):
> "*È ancora stimato uno principe, quando elli è vero amico e vero inimico, cioè quando sanza alcuno respetto si scuopre in favore di alcuno contro ad un altro. Il quale partito fia sempre più utile che stare neutrale: perché, se dua potenti tua vicini vengono alle mani, o sono di qualità che, vincendo uno di quelli, tu abbia a temere del vincitore, o no. In qualunque di questi dua casi, ti sarà sempre più utile lo scoprirti e fare buona guerra.*"
Machiavelli [2006, XXI]

[14] It can be seen in a Pietro Bembo's note commenting Boccaccio's passage in a special edition of *The Decameron* (1555) [Bembo et al., 1555, p. 914]: "*chiunque: maschilmente feminilmente, si dice, chiunque ha neutrale sentimento solamente*".

[15] Hugo Grotius in *De Iure Belli ac Pacis* (1625) uses the term *medium* to mean "neutral": "De his qui in bello medii sunt"; "eorum, qui a bello abstinent officium est [...] aequos se praebere utrisque in permittendo transitu" [Grotius, 1993, III, §17].

"foreign policy", where a certain faction, the "third part", decides to not side in favour of neither of the contenders. Though it doesn't necessarily regard military intervention nor relationships among States or Nations, these factions are always distinct entities which can exert their force or influence in some way. Melians couldn't turn the tide of war, but they could affect the balance of power, if other *poleis* decided to follow the example, remaining neutral and not directly support Athens. Similarly, power games motivated the prince-electors' neutral positions in the dispute between conciliar Fathers and the Pope, during the time of the council of Basel. Anyway, this concept of neutrality is far distant from the liberal one yet. Liberal neutrality determines which space, *inside* the State, shall be conceded to the various conceptions of the good of groups and individuals. The neutral (third) part is the State itself, with its laws and institutions, that is the same entity having monopoly on the use of force, while the contenders are citizens, groups or associations living within the boundaries of the State. This is radically different from the case of a faction choosing to intervene or not in a conflict. Therefore it is needed to examine what is the fundamental passage between the generic conception of neutrality and the one developed within a liberal theory. First, it is clear that without the State (the neutral part) liberal neutrality cannot be: it comes up only with the modern State. However the mere advent of the modern State doesn't explain why it should abstain from siding with a particular faction, instead of using its force to intervene in disputes among parts, imposing a particular policy, culture or religion. The decisive step is the emergence of the concept of tolerance.

1.2   From Toleration to Neutrality

From the XVI to the middle of the XVII century, with the advent of Protestantism, new tensions and conflicts led Europe to be plunged in bloody wars under the guise of religion. The wide spread of the idea of tolerance developed precisely in this framework. There already were much older examples of religious tolerance[16], but in this age it assumes more importance than ever before. The epicentre of these conflicts was the antagonism between German princes and the Hapsburgs Empire. The first claimed their autonomy and the possibility to determine the religion practiced in their lands, while the imperial dynasty wanted to maintain the political unity of the Empire by strengthening its control over German territories, while religious differences could be a highly disruptive force. The casus belli and pretext for the outbreak of the war was thus motivated by religious arguments. The first truce treated between princes and Charles V, king of Spain and Holy Roman Emperor was called Augsburg Peace (1555), with the famous formula *cuius regio, eius religio* ("whose realm, his religion"): the religion of the prince (Catholicism or Lutheranism) became the religion of the State and all its inhabitants. Those inhabitants who could not conform to prince's religion were allowed to leave, an innovative idea in the XVI century. Religious consequences are only one side of the coin: with the right to make this choice, they were actually claiming more autonomy from the Empire, beginning to break its political unity and laying the foundations for the

---

[16] Religion tolerance was adopted in Roman Empire approach to populations made subject. It was a typical concept developed in Neo-Platonism (Themistius from Paphlagonia, Quintus Aurelius Symmachus), but primarily Jews contributed to its spread, claiming to be respected despite their peculiarity (Titus Flavius Josephus). In the early VI century, Cassiodorus and the administration of king Theoderic the Great are good examples of how Christian thought can absorb the ideals of Roman tolerance. See Mauro Pesce's article [2008].

establishment of national States. However when Ferdinand II was crowned, conflicts resumed (Thirty Years War) and lasted until 1648. Clashes of this kind weren't limited to German area, since on another front Netherlands (Calvinist) were fighting for their independence against Ferdinand II, Catholic sovereign of Spain and the Empire. In Europe matters of religion and tolerance are blend in with political conflicts, like the independence wars at the origin of modern State. This is highlighted by Treccani encyclopedia [2009] under the entry "State":

> *"If we look to the internal problems [...] in order to achieve the territoriality of the State, it can be added a new, modern one: the wars of religion, which actually were civil wars. In France the struggle between Catholics and Huguenots (1559-1594); in the Holy Roman Empire - during the Bohemian-Palatine period (1618-1625) of the Thirty Years War - the conflict between Catholics and Protestants; in England the civil war (1640-1649) among Anglicans, Presbyterians, Congregationalists and independents"*
> Treccani Encyclopedia [2009]

The XVI century sees the birth of the modern State, conventionally dated back to the Peace of Westphalia (1648). Simultaneously contractualist thought had origins, with Hobbes' *Leviathan* (1651), and towards the end of the century liberalism, with Locke's political writings. All these developments are connected to each other and it is certainly not a coincidence that Locke, champion of tolerance, is also considered the first liberal thinker[17]. Charles Larmore underlines this aspect:

> *"A century of bloody religious wars was a fact no early liberal thinker could ignore. But this phenomenon is not only a religious one. Over the past four centuries, the nature of the good life in a great many of its aspects has come to seem a topic on which disagreement among reasonable people is not accidental, but to*

---

[17] Michael Zuckert [2002].

expected"
Charles Larmore [1996, 122]

According to Marcello Landi [2005] the idea of tolerance, intended as the fact of tolerating the differences of other people, was born in the modern State characterised by linguistic, juridical and religious homogeneity. It was opposed to the medieval conception of a composite and varied State, since in the modern age differences were seen suspiciously, while during the middle ages they were often seen as a value. A testimony can be found reading the *Corpus iuris Hungarici*, in particular the letter King Stephen (István) of Hungary wrote to his son Emmerich (Imre), dating back to the first half of XI century (between years 1001 and 1038):

> *"When settlers come from different countries and provinces, they bring with them different languages and customs, several things that enhance our culture and armies, which adorn and embellish the royal court, but also scare foreign powers. A land, where there is only one language and one custom, is weak and fragile. Therefore, my son, I assign you the task to meet them and to treat them properly, so that they remain with you more willingly than elsewhere"*
>
> De Werbocz et al. [1779, ch. 6]

In political philosophy the concept of toleration appears by the hands of several authors over the XV and XVI century: Nicholas of Cusa, Marsilio Ficino, Pietro Pomponazzi, Lorenzo Valla, Giordano Bruno and Tommaso Campanella. Jean Bodin, in its *Colloquium Heptaplomeres de Rerum Sublimium Arcanis Abditis* (written in 1588, published only in 1858 and therefore unknown to contemporaries) put in place a dialogue among seven characters, each adhering to a different faith. In the XVII century the idea of tolerance is more popular and goes side by side with political topics, as in authors like Spinoza (*Theological-Political Treatise*, 1670) and Pierre Bayle (*Various Thoughts on the Occasion of a Comet*, 1682). The last expressed the idea, completely innovative, that an atheist government could be fair, or anyway not more vicious than one inspired by religious feelings [Bayle, 1997]. The most famous work is John Locke's *A Letter Concerning Toleration* [1689, a][18]. He states that humans and, in particular, the State, cannot judge the truth claims of different and competing religious views. And even if it could be possible, to impose a single "true" religion would not have the desired effect, since beliefs cannot be imposed by force. The imposition of religious uniformity would result in social unrest to a greater extent than what would follow from a policy that allows diversity. In view of the deepening that will be made in the second chapter, it is worth to already point out that this vision of tolerance is justified more by the pragmatic necessity of ensuring public order and the survival of society, rather than by an underlying moral order[19]. After Locke and during the Enlightenment, the idea of toleration enjoys even a greater diffusion and in Voltaire (*Treatise on Tolerance*, 1763) there is a further development: from being purely a matter of division of powers between the State and the Church, toleration now leads to a reflection on the moral conduct within civil society. Afterwards, all liberal thinkers of the XIX century (like Mill or Tocqueville) and the Founding Fathers of the United States dealt with the notion of toleration. In the XIX and XX century, Nationalisms and various social doctrines (Fascisms, Communism and mass-based parties) imply the necessity to extend the idea of tolerance from a religious dimension to ethnic, social and ideological differences.

---

[18] John Locke, *Epistola de Tolerantia ad Clarissimum Virum* (1689).
[19] This point is raised by Rawls in *Political Liberalism* contesting a vision of neutrality as a *modus vivendi* (see §2.1 of this essay or Rawls [1993, IV, §3]).

1.3   Liberal Neutrality

Many philosophers associate the idea of tolerance developed in the XVII century directly to liberal neutrality. According to Elisabetta Galeotti [1992] neutrality is the tolerance of the age of multiculturalism, while Corrado Del Bò [2011] states that it is simply an extension of the idea of tolerance: today, being conflicts diffused and not polarized as in the past, neutrality does not just apply to a commitment of public authorities to not sanction "heretic" behaviours, as in the XVII century, but goes further and demands equal treatment of various religious, moral and philosophical options in society. It leaves no room for different legal, economic or symbolic treatments. According to Waldron [1993] the concept of neutrality can be already identified in Locke's perspective when he wrote that the sacrifice of calves cannot be prohibited as a religious norm, but may be prohibited for special reasons of safety and public health. In this last case it is not prohibited the sacrifice in itself, but the killing of calves: "law would be made about a political matter, not a religious one" (Locke [1689, a]). This kind of neutrality can be called "neutrality of intentions" or justifications (according to Waldron[20] and Verza [1998])[21], because in the intentions of the government a particular religion and its practices are not questioned, but in actual fact, a neutral approach may imply actions that goes in favour or against a particular religion or a conception of the good life. This approach is divergent from the "neutrality of effects" defined by Joseph Raz (in *The Morality of Freedom* [1986, part II]), who observes that looking at the actual

---

[20] "...the liberal may be talking instead about neutrality of intentions – that is, neutrality in relation to the motives and reasons that the legislator uses to justify his laws" (Waldron [1993, 150]).

[21] According to some authors neutrality of intentions theoretically presents some analytical differences from the neutrality of justification, but in practical application differences are to become opaque. See Corrado del Bò [2011, 6-8].

effects of policies, the State should take care to benefit or disadvantage all conceptions of the good equally. According to this perspective, the State can be neutral only if it creates conditions of equal opportunities such that people are equally free to adopt, and implement their own conception of the good. According to Annalisa Verza [1998] Locke waved between the "neutrality of intentions" and the "neutrality of effects", since in the same passage of *A Letter Concerning Toleration* about killing calves, he specified that the magistrate should always be very cautious in abusing of his authority to coerce some Church under the pretext of the public good.

Both kinds of neutrality require that the justification of a certain action doesn't depend on a certain controversial ideal or religion, but should rely on an independent reason (that is supposed to be shared[22]). This "exclusion of ideals" (as called by Joseph Raz), implying the fact of putting aside particular and controversial commitments while deliberating, involves a sort of "anti-perfectionism". As Rawls states [1971, §50, 286], perfectionism requires to consider the good to be the "achievement of human excellence in art, science and culture" (more generally in all the various forms of culture). If the ruler adopted a perfectionist approach, the policies would likely tend to actively promote his own ideals. Similarly, if the State should promote the ideal of sanctity and spirituality, there would be made policies with the aim of discouraging lustful desires of citizens, supporting in this way the ideal of perfection, or countering imperfection.

A first proposal of neutral political authorities towards moral values can be traced back to Jeremy Bentham's utilitarianism[23]. In *The Rationale of Reward* (1825) he states that "the game of push-pin is of equal value with the arts and sciences of music and poetry", meaning that if the utility produced by playing at

---

[22] This point is highly controversial and will be analysed further in the essay

[23] See the discussion of Bentham's utilitarianism in appendix

push-pin is not less than what produced by poetry, then it's useless to care about the moral value of different sources of utility. Therefore, the political authority has not the purpose nor the right to promote a value or another. This is a first requirement of a minimal State: it should not pursue any controversial conception of good[24]. Charles Larmore says that there are moral conceptions (along with their specific values) that are not controversial, and therefore the State has the right to actively operate in accordance to them. For example, to pursue economic efficiency can be considered as a moral conception, but it is not controversial (Serge Latouche's happy de-growth theory [2011] may oppose productivity, but not efficiency) therefore the State is legitimate to engage this task. The way in which efficiency can be achieved is highly controversial and libertarians believe the intervention of the State is detrimental to efficiency, but this doesn't mean that State and institutions shouldn't enter into the discussion about what is the best way to reach efficiency.

Neutrality towards conflicting moral values is not reduced to utilitarianism, nor necessarily depends on that doctrine. The idea of liberal neutrality is simply "non-perfectionist", in the sense that it entrusts the moral perfection to the voluntary decisions of individuals in society, who are then free to choose which ideal to follow. The problem arises when applying neutrality of intentions we obtain a non-equal effect towards different conceptions of good. In this case neutrality of intentions conflicts with neutrality of effects. As it has been said, neutrality of intentions relies on a justification that is a reason independent from controversial values (like the ideal of sanctity of Christian faith), then to justify neutrality we should provide a "public

---

[24] Anthony de Jasay [1991] associates Bentham's utilitarianism to liberal neutrality

reason"[25], that is an argument characterised by political values, that are supposed to be independent from any comprehensive doctrine or conception of the good (from any kind of "faith"). In this case we can consider "public" as a synonym of "independent". The prohibition of killing calves, in Locke's example, is supported by the neutral State not because it is a sacrifice (that should be allowed as any other manifestation of religious values), but because of an independent reason, like the need to not further reduce the size of herds already decimated by an epidemic. Robert Nozick tries to outline the notion of "independent reason" in the following passage. This fragment probably also contains one of the very first appearances of the term "neutrality" in political philosophy associated to a conception of liberal State:

> *"Not every enforcement of a prohibition which differentially benefits people makes the state non-neutral. Suppose some men are potential rapists of women, while no women are potential rapists of men or of each other. Would a prohibition against rape be non-neutral? It would, by hypothesis, differentially benefit people; but for potential rapists to complain that the prohibition was non-neutral between the sexes, and therefore sexist, would be absurd. There is an independent reason for prohibiting rape: people have a right to control their own bodies, to choose their sexual partners, and to be secure against physical force and its threat. That a prohibition thus independently justifiable works out to affect different persons differently is no reason to condemn it as non-neutral [...] To claim that a prohibition or rule is non-neutral presupposes that it is unfair"*
> Robert Nozick [1974, 272-273]

---

[25] The ideal of public reason does hold for citizens when they engage in political advocacy in the public forum, and is used by John Rawls in *Political Liberalism* [1993, VI, §1.1, 214] to indicate in a democratic society "the reason of equal citizens who, as a collective body, exercise final political and coercive power over one another in enacting laws and in amending their constitution".

Neutrality of justifications presupposes the distinction between what is not legitimately pursued at political level, from what is considered "fair" or "just". It is clear that it's not possible to arbitrarily decide if a justification (or reason) is independent and, consequently, which prohibitions the State is legitimated to impose, or which policies shall be adopted. In Nozick's passage above, what is neutral is even fair, and vice versa. According to him, for the case above the independent (neutral) reason is simply justified thanks to the principle stating that "people have a right to control their own bodies". The problem is that even this principle of self-ownership may be considered controversial and may involve a particular and controversial conception of good life. According to some authors, like Michael Sandel[26], we cannot leave aside our own values in order to deliberate in a neutral way, that is, we cannot disregard our personal comprehensive doctrine in order to identify an independent reason. In this perspective, no reason is independent at all, then no "public reason" can actually be "independent". Despite this, there are authors who tried to outline a theory of justice in which the fundamental principles are independent, or neutral, towards the conceptions of the good. John Rawls in *A Theory of Justice* made a big effort in this direction.

1.4   Neutrality in Rawls' Perspective

As it has been said, utilitarianism may lead to a conception of the State that is anti-perfectionist, because satisfaction is something subjective and institutions cannot establish which value maximizes individual utility. Utilitarianism requires that institutions are "arranged so as to achieve the greatest net balance of satisfaction summed over all the individuals" (Rawls

---

[26] Sandel's perspective will be further analysed in paragraph 1.5

[1971, §5, 20]). But as noted by Villani [1988], all utilitarians (except Bentham), tended to weigh individual preferences, defining legitimate and illegitimate interests of citizens, before to include them in the "social calculation"; this inevitably implies an appeal to comprehensive doctrines. The reason is that utilitarianism is a teleological doctrine: "the good is defined independently from the right, and then the right is defined as that which maximizes the good"[27]. If institutions considered holiness as the only value yielding satisfaction, in order to maximize this conception of the good the rules (defining a conception of the right) would probably appeal to a controversial doctrine, like Christian social doctrine. Contrary to utilitarianism, Rawls defines the right as prior to the good, and this outlook represents a more promising way in which the State can be neutral towards different conceptions of good life. He introduces the notion of "pure procedural justice": "there is a correct or fair procedure such that the outcome is likewise correct or fair, whatever it is, provided that the procedure has been properly followed" (Rawls [1971, §14, 75]). Gambling is an example of pure procedural justice: assuming that fair bets are those having a zero expectation of gain, that the bets are made voluntarily and that no one cheats (these assumptions establish the procedure), any final distribution of cash at the end of the game is equally fair if the procedure is followed properly. The good (a particular distribution of cash) is therefore defined as the result of a fair, or just, procedure.

In *A Theory of Justice* the pure procedural justice is represented by the original position: principles of justice are the result of an agreement among people placed in an imaginary situation (a typical *gedankenexperiment*): the "original position". Individuals in this particular situation have no information about their own

---

[27] Here Rawls [1971, §5, 22] adopts W. K. Frankena's definition of teleological theories in *Ethics* (Englewood Cliffs, N.J., Prentice Hall, Inc., 1963), p. 13

present or future place and identity in society: for example they don't know anything about their own talents and abilities, social status, physical characteristics, religion and conceptions of the good. This condition is called "veil of ignorance". Thus in the original position people deliberate in a perfectly symmetric position, as if they all were equal. No one can take personal advantage over others, in choosing whatever criterion of justice. It is important to specify that the parts in original position shall conceive themselves as members of a "well-ordered society"[28]. It means that the principles established in original position shall constitute the grounds of a well-ordered society (in this sense, the notion of original position has no significance without the one of well-ordered society), a society in which we would like to live, at least in which all "reasonable" people (according to Rawls) would like to live. The notion of "reasonable" has normative implication in Rawls' theory: it is possible to say that only the people who accept the condition of the well-ordered society are reasonable. In that kind of society all members "accept and know that all the others accept the same political conception of justice" (Rawls [2001, §3.2, 9]) and institutions satisfy the principles of justice given by that shared political conception. Moreover, all members see themselves as endowed with a right to equal respect and consideration[29]. But it is not a mere utopistic society, it also displays features that are common to all actual modern society: there is divergence in fundamental interests and purposes, and a variety of incompatible beliefs. Therefore all members cannot accept the same comprehensive doctrine, but they may agree on a political conception of justice. Rawls explains [1974] that those who feel no affinity for the

---

[28] All features of a well-ordered society were first displayed in *Reply to Alexander and Musgrave* [1974]. Here the references are taken from *Justice as Fairness* [2001], which includes the notions of the preceding essay.
[29] "All who can be fully cooperating members of political society count as equals and can be treated differently only as the public political conception of justice allows" (Rawls [2001, §7.3, 21])

notion of a well-ordered society (people who are not reasonable) will remain indifferent to justice as fairness, since its conditions are not morally neutral: "the conception of the person as free and equal is a normative conception" [2001, §7.6, 24]. It means that Rawls' theory of justice as fairness endorse a particular conception of the good, then it is morally non-neutral. Nonetheless, this political (and moral) conception is non-controversial, since as Rawls himself specifies in *Political liberalism* [1999, §6, 39] it is shared by all the "reasonable but opposing comprehensive doctrines" (and society would remain well-ordered until "unreasonable comprehensive doctrines do not gain enough currency to undermine society's essential justice"). The agreement among reasonable parties give raise to the principles of justice, constituting the basic structure of society (that comes before the constitution and can be considered as a sort of preamble[30]).

The consensus on the conditions established by the idea of a well-ordered society, shared by all reasonable doctrine, is referred to as "overlapping consensus". Given this framework on which each reasonable person agrees, the original position and the veil of ignorance ensure the principles – resulting from the agreement – to be necessarily equal and just (on the basis of pure procedural justice criterion). Thus the equal conditions of the contractors allow to build an order that can be object of stable consensus among the parts, each one characterised by its own comprehensive doctrine. But to produce that order there's no need to draw on any of the controversial features belonging to the reasonable comprehensive doctrines. Here comes the idea of neutrality, although Rawls in 1971 still does not explicitly treat that topic. Critics and followers will detect first this concept in

---

[30] "it might be accepted as one of society's political aspirations in a preamble that lacks legal force (as with the U.S. Constitution)" (Rawls [2001, §49.5, 162])

his philosophy, until Rawls recognizes it in *Political Liberalism* (1993)[31].

Pure procedural justice is a way to define principles of justice, but only among "reasonable" people, that is, people who agree on the moral requirements incorporated in the notion of well-ordered society. As a result, they accept to place themselves in the original position to choose the principles of justice. It has been said, the notion of "reasonable" is normative, implying the moral conception of the person as free and equal (Rawls [1993, III, §1.2, 94]), then the notion of "reasonable" is based on a particular ideal of equality. The best way to grasp the idea of "reasonable" is not provided by John Rawls, and it is unfortunate, since it should have been essential to his theory of justice as fairness. Charles Larmore's discussion of equal respect will serve this purpose, as it will be explained in the second chapter.

At a first glance we might think of utilitarianism as the most rational conception of justice. It requires that institutions achieve the greatest net balance of satisfaction summed over all the individuals. Since in realizing our own interests we are free to balance our own losses against our own gains, we may rationally impose a sacrifice on ourselves now for the sake of a greater advantage later. Under a utilitarian perspective, society would act on precisely the same principle applied to the group, therefore regarding that which is rational for one man as right for an association of men. In this way, it allows to sacrifice the welfare of some individuals in order to advance as far as possible the welfare of the group (Rawls [1971, §5, 21]). Then Rawls concludes that utilitarianism "does not take seriously the distinction between persons" [1971, §5, 24].[32]

---

[31] In Lecture V "Priority of Right and Ideas of the Good", in particular §5 "Permissible Conceptions of the Good and Political Virtues" (Rawls [1993])

[32] A further discussion on these issues can be found in the appendix

Contrary to utilitarianism, which relies on a "single-principle conception" with one ultimate standard (the maximization of welfare), intuitionism requires a family of principles which have to be weighed against one another. While the complexity of the moral facts requires a number of distinct principles, there is no single standard that accounts for them or assigns them their weights (Rawls [1971, §7, 30]). It means that intuitionism includes no explicit method, nor priority rules, for weighing these principles against one another. This conception of justice imposes no limitations on what are the correct weightings, allowing different persons to arrive at a different balance of principles [1971, §7, 34]. The intuitionist hopes that once principles are identified, we will in fact balance them more or less similarly, at least if we are impartial and not moved by an excessive attention to our own interests. Or if this is not so, then at least we can agree to some scheme whereby our assignment of weights can be compromised. Nonetheless, what Rawls underlines is that we cannot assume that our intuitive judgments of priority will in general be the same; given our different positions in society they surely will not. Thus Rawls supposes parties in the original position try to reach some agreement as to how the principles of justice are to be balanced, providing a serial or lexical order which requires us to satisfy the first principle in the ordering before we can move on to the second, the second before we consider the third, and so on [1971, §8, 37]. In addressing the "priority problem" the task is that of reducing and not of eliminating entirely the reliance on intuitive judgments. Thus our object should be to formulate a conception of justice which tends to make our considered judgments of justice converge [1971, §8, 39-40]. In this way Rawls formulates two fundamental principles, the first prior to the second:

> *"First: each person is to have an equal right to the most extensive scheme of equal basic liberties compatible with a similar scheme of liberties for others.*

> *Second: social and economic inequalities are to be arranged so that*
> *they are both (a) reasonably expected to be to everyone's advantage,*
> *and (b) attached to positions and offices open to all"*
> John Rawls [1971, §11, 53]

Rawls later specifies [§46, 266] that the point (a) refers to "the greatest benefit of the least-advantaged" (members of the society): this coincides with the difference principle. These principles aim at regulating a problem of distributive justice: they establish how citizens benefit from the allocation of rights, duties and social or economic benefits. In order to measure the "benefits" the notion of "utility" as welfare typical of utilitarian theories is rejected, preferring instead the notion of "primary goods", that are, in short, "rights, liberties, and opportunities, and income and wealth" [1974, §11, 54]. The index of primary goods is "an index of expectations of these goods over the course of a complete life" [2001, §51.5, 172]. Expectations are not constituted by the satisfaction people presume to obtain by means of the goods at their disposal. If thought in this way, the index would take into account all the comprehensive conceptions of the good citizens adhere to. Primary goods are not determined on the basis of how much satisfaction they bring when employed, nor they identify any specific conception of the good. They are the means everybody can use (or not use, if they prefer) in order to pursue their own conception of the good (cf *Theory* [1971, §15, 80-81]. In the third chapter the principles of justice and the concept of primary goods are analysed in depth and it will be explained why can actually be considered neutral towards comprehensive doctrines.

1.5   The Communitarian Critique

In the Seventies Rawls opens the way to several philosophers who highlighted the importance of the notion of neutrality.

Besides Nozick in 1971 with *Anarchy, State, and Utopia*, a group of authors made an analytical study of the concept of neutrality in the collective book *Neutrality and Impartiality: The University and Political Commitment* (1975), edited by Montefiore. However the most relevant contribution is given by communitarian authors, like Michael Sandel [1982], who moves criticism against Rawls' neutral perspective. Though Rawls didn't expressly deal with neutrality before *Political liberalism* (1993), the concept Sandel rails against was already present in *A Theory of Justice* and is well defined by Dworkin [1985, 181] in this way: "government must be neutral on what might be called the question of the good life. [...] political decisions must be, so far as is possible, independent of any particular conception of the good life, or of what gives value to life". According to liberal theories, since no comprehensive conception of good life is sharable, in order to regulate the relationship between individuals and to protect their (individual) purposes, it is necessary to share neutral and impersonal principles of justice. Thus justice becomes the first virtue of liberal institutions, implying the priority of right on the good. According to Sandel, Rawls' social contract, based on the priority of the right and the principle of neutrality, is unfeasible since citizens cannot disregard the moral roots given by their traditions, which directly shape the conceptions of the good of citizens. Therefore an imaginary contract has no meaning in practice, since it is stipulated among citizens placed in a totally abstract and "counterfactual" situation, like the original position. The community represents a world of values that exists independently from the will of individuals and their rational choices, only within a community individuals acquire conscience of what are their own duties and what are the purposes to which conform their choices. Liberalism cannot properly give raise to the value of this fundamental bond between individual and social sphere. Citizens should mutually recognize their membership in political communities characterized by common traditions and a sense of collective belonging. In the second chapter (§2.5) the controversy between Sandel and Rawls will be analysed further, introducing some remarkable observations made by Charles Larmore, who refers to the communitarian objection to liberalism as "the Romantic critique of modern individualism".

Michael Walzer's criticism [1987] is not distant from Sandel's observations. He opposes the liberal idea of justice as universal value, unrelated to the specific contexts of different societies. Rawls would try to give "a universal corrective for all the different social moralities", thus liberalism cannot offer to members of a community what they really want, that is "a dense moral culture within which they can feel some sense of belonging". The formulation of the principles of justice may be presented as requiring to people to conceive justice as the construction of a sort of hotel, in which "if there were luxury suites, their only purpose would be to bring more business to the hotel and enable us to improve all the other rooms, starting with those most in need of improvement" (Walzer [1987, 14]). Here Walzer refers in particular to the difference principle. Nonetheless, if we were to take a hotel room as the ideal model of a human home, "we might still long for the homes we knew we once had but could no longer remember. We would not be morally bound to live in the hotel we had designed" [1987, 15]. According to Walzer, Rawls embarks on the "path of invention", designing a new moral world, like a new language, but there is "no divine or natural blueprint to guide" the designer. Then the "crucial requirement of a design procedure is that it eventuate in agreement". The problem is that the new moral has significance only for the designer himself, it cannot be universal and no agreement is possible: "Why should newly invented principles govern the lives of people who already share a moral culture and speak a natural language?" [1987, 10, 12]. Moral argument rather than "inventive" should be "interpretative", "closely resembling the work of a lawyer or judge who struggles to find meaning in a morass of conflicting laws and precedents" [1987, 19]. Morality cannot be constructed or invented, it is "something we have to argue about. The argument implies common possession, but common possession does not imply agreement [...] No discovery or invention can end the argument" [1987, 29]. The same concepts, if referred to a political or economic distributive issue, imply that the goods to distribute are expression of social needs, shared by the community on the basis of a concrete identity of its members. Therefore, to determine what is a fair distribution, it is necessary to consider the specific situation of a given society, it is not possible to apply universal norms (cf Walzer [1983]).

Similar criticism appears in Charles Taylor, who emphasizes the problem of the moral foundation of the rights. The rights of citizens shouldn't be founded on universalistic claims, rather they find justification on the ground of belonging to a specific community. In this perspective, the "common good" prevail on the right and overrides the primacy given by liberalism to a "neutral" sense of justice[33].

During the Eighties the theme of neutrality is at the centre of the debate between liberals and communitarians. As it has been exposed, the communitarian focused against the idea of the "priority of right on good" presented in *A Theory of Justice*, according to which there is a correct or fair (neutral) procedure "such that the outcome is likewise correct or fair, whatever it is, provided that the procedure has been properly followed" [1971, §14 86]. Rawls' answer is provided in *Political Liberalim* (1993), where he states that such procedure cannot abstract from moral values: as a matter of fact to demonstrate that something is justified implies necessarily an appeal to certain values, that are not left aside in a liberal theory, as communitarians believed. Neutrality itself cannot explain why a neutral decision is actually

---

[33] See also Maria Dodaro [2011, 151].

better than a partisan one, nor why authority shouldn't support one party as well as its claims prevail on the other ones without any moral justification, but only thanks to its power, for instance. Then neutrality needs to be justified somehow: disagreeing parties should share a common moral ground that is, in other words, the "overlapping consensus". As Rawls says, this consensus is constituted by "fundamental intuitive ideas implicit in the public political culture and abstracting from comprehensive religious, philosophical, and moral doctrines. It seeks common ground – or if one prefers, neutral ground" [1993, V, §5, 192]. Charles Larmore makes explicit these ideas "implicit in the public political culture": they are the "rational dialogue" (purely procedural) and the "equal respect" (moral), and will be explained carefully in the second chapter. Larmore's answer to the long-debated question among liberals and communitarians is precisely the principle of equal respect, which – in brief – requires us to discuss in a rational way with those showing their disposition to discuss in a rational way with us. The goal of political liberalism is to refute the claim "that liberalism makes sense only as affirmation of individualistic views about the good life", instead, it "seeks to detach the principle of political neutrality from the fate of this view" explaining why liberalism is not a force "that work against the Romantic values of belonging and tradition" (Larmore [1996, 151]. Though equal respect prescribes a neutral procedure of deliberation (the rational dialogue), it is a moral concept that is not built (or invented) in a constructivist way. Michael Walzer would have said that it can be identified through the path of "moral interpretation", not "moral invention". Larmore, making reference to the historical roots of western modern societies, explains why the dominant tradition of the western modern political culture should acknowledge equal respect as a political ideal. The fact that both liberals and communitarians cannot find a valid reason to reject this principle is due to particular features of our modern society, influenced by history and historical development of philosophical and political thinking. The first and most important of these features is the heterogeneity of moral thinking: it happens when different structures of moral order collide and there's no possibility to find a solution. The acknowledgment of an heterogeneous moral order leads to the acceptance of pluralism.

1.6   Pluralism and Heterogeneity of Morality

It has been said in paragraph 1.2 that during the middle ages cultural differences were already seen as a value. This can lead to think that pluralism isn't a distinctive feature of modernity. Actually, pluralism isn't anything new, but Charles Larmore underlines that the innovative character of modernity is the progressive importance of pluralism that becomes *central*, rather than being a merely marginal matter. This is due to harsh internal conflicts and civil wars in the name of religion that never had such resonance before.

> "*More than a century of religious civil war led seventeenth century thinkers such as Locke (as it had already led sixteenth century thinkers like Bodin) to insist upon two distinct but interrelated ideas that never played more than a minor role in ancient and medieval thought. One was the* pluralist *conviction that there exist many differente but independently and even equally valuable conceptions of the good life; the other was the need for* toleration *because reasonable people are likely to disagree about what belongs to the good life*"
> Charles Larmore [1987, xii]

Centrality of tolerance and pluralism is an innovation of Modern age. The difference between them is that while tolerance concerns a *disagreement* about ideals (and the acceptance of this disagreement), pluralism has to do with the *agreement* about the

31

fact that there are different ideals of "independent and equal value" [1987, xii-xiii]. According to Larmore, pluralism "is a truth we should accept" [1996, 153], but it still seems controversial when is meant like a "doctrine", as Isaiah Berlin outlined: life affords a plurality of values "equally objective" and "there are many objective ends, ultimate values, some incompatible with other" [1991, 79-80]. Political liberalism isn't based on the acceptance of pluralism as an ideal, nor demands that its virtues must be promoted, nor requires that everyone should pursue her own aims and values. This means that we are not required to endorse the relativistic idea that there cannot be a unique truth, since the acceptance of pluralism as a doctrine is irrelevant. On the contrary, the mere existence of pluralism justifies liberal ideals: citizens will never agree on a unique truth. According to Larmore, in western modern society the existence of pluralism is simply a matter of fact.

> *"This expectation of reasonable disagreement, to which liberalism does appeal, lies at a different, one might almost say more "impartial", level than pluralism. It responds to the idea of a religiously and metaphysically disenchanted world not by affirming it, as pluralism seems to do, but rather by recognizing that like other deep conceptions of value this disenchantment is an idea about which reasonable people are likely to disagree"*
> Charles Larmore [1996, 167-168]

Disenchantment about a final truth in religious and metaphysical sphere leads to the expectation of reasonable disagreement in the sense that, in our society, reasonable people wouldn't expect to agree upon a unique truth, even if they believe in the existence of a unique truth. It is a factual condition, and a prerequisite in order to legitimate the existence of different conceptions in people's moral (and ultimately the norm of equal respect).

According to Larmore, before thinkers like Bodin or Locke, reigned unchallenged the axiom that reason leads to unanimity. Moral conflict seemed always to have been a mark of our ignorance, not a reflection of the moral order. Reason may fail and generate dissent, but only because of lack of knowledge. In *Patterns of Moral Complexity* Larmore explains that this *monistic* conception of ethical theory (precisely in opposition to pluralism), derives from Aristotle and his dissertation, in *The Nicomachean Ethics*, about φρόνησις (*phronesis*), that is moral *judgement*. He highlights the role of examples in moral deliberation, because moral judgement is not governed by general rules, concerning rather the peculiarity of the situation. According to Aristotle the virtue doesn't consist exclusively in the knowledge of general principles (or rules), but is rather the application of principles to particular circumstances. This is the doctrine of the *mean* (cf Larmore [1987, 15-16]), that stands beyond two corresponding faults or vices, which consist respectively of the excess and the deficiency of something of which the virtue represents the right amount. It can't be calculated through the use of general rules, rather is a mean "relative to us". Then the moral judgement must always suit the particularity of circumstances and can be learned only through practice. Because "training and experience play such a vital role in the acquisition of judgement, the development of moral character depends upon the moral life of the community" and ultimately, virtue depends on belonging (Larmore [1987, 15]). This argument is precisely what neo-aristotelian political philosophers have in common with communitarians.

Larmore recognize the centrality of *judgement*, that was instead disregarded by modern ethics, but at the same time he opposes neo-aristotelian tendencies, like what MacIntyre's represented in *After Virtue* (1981), because antagonistic to political liberalism, as "MacIntyre well intends it to be" (Larmore [1987, 22]). Larmore wants to prove that throughout history the abandonment of an Aristotelian conception of morality, which hinges on the central role of the examples and *judgment*, leads to the formation of the distinctive character of modernity: the ethics of pluralism. Aristotelian's outlook is opposed to the view – advanced by

Immanuel Kant – that examples are extrinsic to moral order, because they are no more than the simple application of the rule to a particular case. According to Kant[34], the best way to think of concepts is as rules. For example, the concept "table" should be construed as the rule we employ for classifying certain things as tables[35]. Then *judgement* enables us to realize that "a thing falls within the scope of a rule". This faculty can be improved through the use of examples – examples of the rules being applied in concrete case – but they are merely rhetorical means, having the only purpose of motivating us[36]; they don't have any logical purpose, instead, as in the doctrine of the *mean*.

According to Larmore, this is the dominant perspective of modern ethics. At this point, the critical step to deal with is how this vision, in which morality is simply the application of the rule, leads inevitably to a pluralistic perspective. Often it happens that we invoke different rules, so that it is not possible to decide among rival claims anymore. We can't exercise *judgement* in order to decide which is the right action in a certain situation, for the rule does not take into account circumstances (think of the categorical imperative). This is a form of moral conflict typical of Modern age, because dissent doesn't originate due to lack of knowledge, but because of the heterogeneous moral order itself. This may happen even for inner conflicting thoughts, moreover when we have different persons in conflict.

In classical ethics, all moral conflicts were supposed to have a solution. In fact monism, which is precisely the opposite of pluralism, was the dominant pattern of moral thought in ancient Greek. Conflicts generated within monistic vision of morality

---

[34] Larmore [1987, 2] refers here to the *Critique of Pure Reason*.

[35] This conception may recall Plato's ideal of Hyperuranion, the realm of archetypal ideas. According to Larmore, Aristotle opposed Plato's belief that virtue consists solely in the knowledge of general principles, exactly like Kant [1987, 15].

[36] Larmore [1990, 1-2] refers here to the *Grounwork of the Metaphyisics of Moral*.

could be resolved thanks to the commensurability of antagonistic values: a comparison could be possible due to the existence of a unique measure and source of value which represented a common basis to determine the weight of moral conflicting duties or ideals (Larmore [1996, 156-157]). There were no conflicts between different comprehensive conceptions of the good, nor between forms of moral reasoning such as consequentialism and deontology (that will be discussed in next paragraph). Under a pluralistic perspective, there are conflicts without solution either because we do not yet have the information needed to resolve them, or because we think no information will ever be uncovered about how to decide the issue (this last case is the truly irresolvable conflict). Yet, MacIntyre [1981] states that the Greeks of classical time were already conscious of the possibility of moral conflicts that do not admit rational solution, as demonstrated by pre-classical heroic ethic of Aeschylus' *Oresteia*. Furthermore, conflicts between pre-classical and classical ethic were already recognized, as Sophocles presented in *Antigone:* the dispute between Antigone and Creon, which Hegel represented as the conflict among Family and State, the divine (and private) law, typical of pre-classical ethic, against the human law, typical of classical ethic[37]. The divine verdict (*deus ex machina*) always ends rather than resolving the conflict. MacIntyre is considered one of the foremost exponents of neo-

---

[37] In Sophocles' *Antigone*, Creon, king of Thebes, prohibited Polynices' burial , since he was considered a traitor, while gave Eteocles (brother of Polynices) honourable burial. Their sister Antigone couldn't permit Polynices' body be unburied, then symbolically threw a handful of dust above his body. The conflict between Antigone and Creon represents private reasons (to bury the brother) against the reason of the State, as well as divine law against human law. The first, so-called αγραπτα νομιμα (*corpus* of customary laws, considered of divine origin, the prerogative of the *genos*) are affirmed by Antigone, while Creon relies on the νομος (*corpus* of the laws of *polis*). In the rival claims of Antigone and Creon, Hegel sees the conflict between Family and State (*Lectures on Aesthetics*).

Aristotelianism in moral and political philosophy[38], but in spite of this, he unexpectedly criticizes Aristotle for thinking that man will never face irresolvable moral conflicts: the hero of MacIntiyre's book "turns out to be not Aristotle but Sophocles, precisely because Sophocles recognized that there are rationally interminable moral conflicts" (Larmore [1987, 38]). At the end, according to Larmore even MacIntyre embraces a pluralist outlook. However, even if in pre-modern times there were exponents of pluralism, it remains a distinctively modern doctrine, together with relativism: a plural outlook "belongs to a disenchanted vision of the world, which sees itself has having abandoned the comfort of finding in the harmony of the cosmos or in God's providential ordering of the world the one ultimate source of value" (Larmore [1996, 164]).

1.7   Deontology and Consequentialism

The clash between Kantian and Aristotelian ethic is an example of different and conflicting moral orders, the first is the archetype of a deontological order, the second a consequentialistic one. According to Larmore a deontological outlook involves "a set of absolute duties we must heed whatever others may do as a result of what we do" [1987, xi], while a consequentialist outlook demands "that we bring about the greatest good overall, so that what we ought to do depends on how we expect others to react to what we do" (the foreseeable consequences). It may happen that in western modern societies these different "structures" of thought (deontology and consequentialism) coexist, thanks to our particular history. An example of deontology is well represented by the Ten Commandments in Christian doctrine, as well as by

---

[38] See Larmore [1987, 22]),

the Kantian categorical imperative, while utilitarianism is clearly a consequentialistic ethic.

Before to proceed in the analysis, it is necessary to explain why it has been chosen the notion of consequentialism, rather than that of teleology, as opposed to a deontological ethic. According to Massimo Reichlin [2008] there are two kinds of teleological approaches, "consequentialist" and "non-consequentialist". The distinction between teleology and deontology loses its significance if we consider the non-consequentialist teleology. Reichlin provides an example regarding the rule "you shall not kill": under a deontological perspective it has an intrinsic value, while under a teleological perspective its significance lies upon the purpose of promoting the value of life. A teleological ethic may therefore justify some exception to that rule, for example to kill a terrorist might promote the value of life because in consequence of our action the number of saved lives would be greater. Nonetheless, a teleological doctrine may even oppose the action of killing, without exceptions. In this case, the fact of being a murderer (even when killing a terrorist) wold be considered a more serious crime than letting a terrorist to commit a massacre (if he is left alive). In this last case, non-consequentialist teleological ethic establish a hierarchy of values, refusing the full commensurability among them (it doesn't matter how many people the terrorist would kill), though the rightness of acts depends always and solely on its consequences. In this case a teleological ethic may be similar to a deontological one, since it also present a "form of moral absolutism". According to Reichlin, Aristotle in *Nicomachean Ethic* endorses explicitly the existence of acts that cannot be justified in any way at all, therefore his perspective fits this last kind of teleology. Yet, there are other versions of teleological ethics, like utilitarianism, that are consequentialistic: whatever action may be justified on the basis of its consequences in particular circumstances. The term consequentialism and its distinction from teleological perspectives are introduced by Elizabeth Anscombe in *Modern Moral Philosophy* (1958), while a distinction between utilitarianism and deontology was already proposed by Bentham in *An Introduction to the Principles of Morals and Legislation* (1789).

According to Larmore none of the different and conflicting moral patterns (deontology and consequentialism) should be rejected, so it's necessary to let them coexist and to face related arising conflicts, often irresolvable. Max Weber agreed with this idea and treated it in the conference about political *beruf* in 1919 [1994, 359-360], distinguishing between the "ethic of conviction" (deontology, even called "ethic of the rights") and the "ethic of responsibility" (consequentialism, or "ethic of the good"); these ethics are both valid and often they may lead to an hardly (or impossibly) resolvable conflict:

> *"A syndicalist who is committed to the ethics of conviction might be fully aware that the likely consequences of his actions will be, say, increased chances for the forces of reaction, increased oppression of his own class, a brake on the rise of his class. [...] If evil consequences flow from an action done out of pure conviction, this type of person holds the world, not the doer, responsible, or the stupidity of others, or the will of God who made them thus. A man who subscribes to the ethic of responsibility, by contrast [...] has no right, as Fichte correctly observed, to presuppose goodness and perfection in human beings. He does not feel that he can shuffle off the consequences of his own actions, as far as he could foresee them, and place the burden on the shoulders of others. [...] The person who subscribes to the ethic of conviction feels «responsible» only for ensuring that the flame of pure conviction (for example, the flame of protest against the injustice of the social order) is never extinguished. To kindle that flame again and again is the purpose of his actions, actions which, judged from the point of view of their possible success, are utterly irrational, and which can and are only intended to have exemplary value"*
> Max Weber [1994, 360]

MacIntyre states that there is a fundamental difference between Sophocles and modern thinkers endorsing a pluralist outlook, like Weber or Berlin, because they do not conceive conflicts as *tragic*, while Sophocles considers the possibility of discarding one of the alternatives in conflict only by regret, since it still has a claim on us. According to Larmore, MacIntyre's argument "could not be more unfair" [1987, 38-39], because Weber knows very well that different values may be antagonist but equally important and is conscious of the moral costs that pursuing a particular value (neglecting another) may implicate.

The idea of the priority of right over the good can be understood as the priority of a deontological ethic over a consequentialist ethic. In modern era rules (the right) become predominant primarily through the development of Christian theology: this process clearly anticipates what Kant would have stated centuries later. Duns Scoto in the XIII century argued that "the Christian rule of loving others for their own sake and thus a real sense of justice (*affection justitiae*) cannot draw on the natural desire of self-perfection which, as he observed, underlies Aristotelian and Thomistic ethics [...]. Christian theology [...] played an indispensable role in the rise of an ethics of the right" (Larmore [1996, 22]). Later, Kant is the first in formulating the concept of the priority of right on good, in the *Critique of Practical Reason:* "the concept of good and evil is not defined prior to the moral law [...] rather the concept of good and evil must be defined after and by means of the law" (see Larmore [1996, 21]). But in *Morals of Modernity* Larmore states that is not the deontological priority of right itself to be the very fundamental feature of modernity. What is central in modern era, and what Kantian philosophy highlights, is the independence of moral duties from the own good of the agent pursuing such duties. This is a feature displayed in modernity even by utilitarianism, that is consequentialist, not only by deontological outlooks. In fact utilitarianism defines the good by considering impartially the total good of all persons involved, each of them counting as one and only one, independently from whatever the interest of the agent would be. This is the very innovative feature of modernity. Once the right is made prior to the good, Hegel explains that we may expect to find ourselves in a situation where what we ought to do (according to a deontological ethic) is in opposition to what we want to do, and this conflict do not disappear in light of a deeper understanding of what we really want, as it happened in ancient times (cf Larmore [1996, 23]). If self-fulfilment gives precedence to moral claims, it means that we have internalized these claims and we live "under the authority of conscience". This generates a "duality" in our inner moral reasoning: between what Sidgwick in *The Methods of Ethics* called the *imperative* conception (priority of right) and *attractive* conception (priority of the good of the agent) (see Larmore [1996, 20]).

One last fundamental passage in order to understand the affirmation of pluralism and modern ethic is the development of nihilist and relativist perspectives. In *Morals of Modernity* Larmore devotes an entire chapter to Nietzsche, mentioning many interpretations of the German philosopher that were developing during the XX century, just to conclude that "almost every one of these interpretations is as good as the others, except insofar as it claims to be the right one. Only when we have grasped this will we have understood Nietzsche's true legacy. [...] There are no facts, only interpretations" [1996, pag. 81]. But Nietzsche didn't deny (like Berkeley does) a world distinct from minds and the perspectives they project, nor he held that we should adopt the opposing view (like Foucault or Derrida do) that there are no authors, only texts. Both of them are only *interpretations*, and we shouldn't necessarily embrace them (see Larmore [1996, 82]). Similarly, acknowledging the heterogeneity of the moral order doesn't require that we hold the doctrine of pluralism as Berlin proposed, which means that we believe there are different values "equally objective", since it is only another interpretation.

Relativism is not an indispensable requisite of political liberalism. We can still believe in the existence of a unique truth. Acknowledging the heterogeneity of morality implies simply that we understand conflicts may have no solution: various interpretations cannot be redeemed to a unique perspective, and disagreement will always last.

There are even political, rather than philosophical, reasons for the growth of deontology in moral thought: in particular the demands of the modern democracy, that were going to develop since the XVI century. As Larmore explains, in *Patterns of Moral Complexity* [1987, 16], in the modern era "the technical construal of morality ensured that the moral life would be equally accessible to all, and not tied to some inscrutable know-how of the aristocracy". The clearly defined rules, typical of a deontological perspective, are a suitable instrument for this purpose: "This was a worthy political end (for judgment is not the peculiar property of any class)" [1987, 16-17]. In fact, modern democracy demands that all citizens must be placed in the conditions of participating to public deliberations. Therefore, they must be aware of the motivations that lead to the moral choices of political institutions, because only in this way they can express their own opinion through the vote. Otherwise, political elites might exclude the rest of citizens from political participation, justifying public choices by moral arguments that for their complexity would be inaccessible to the majority of the population. Therefore democracy demands a partial abandonment of *judgment* (Aristotelian *phronesis*) in favour of a deontological perspective which gives priority to the scrupulous compliance to rules. Larmore stresses even negative effects of this aspect of modernity, recognizing some positive features of the Aristotelian ethic. In fact the mere rules of modern deontological ethics may disregard the complexity of the studied phenomena. But in some circumstances paying attention to this complexity may be inopportune as well: a modern State must pursue the ideal of "predictability" so that citizens can feel themselves free. Everyone, foreseeing what the government would do, can plan her life and take the right precautions. An investor prefers to know how the central bank disposes the money supply instead of knowing if, whatever choice will be, it will be morally correct. On the contrary, a state of uncertainty does not guarantee freedom. Therefore, instead of political elites who govern by uncodified know-how (that is, through complex moral judgement, rather than public statutes), we still may prefer elites who govern on the basis of precise directives, corresponding to our ethical principles only in a blurred way, provided that predictability is secured. Bureaucracy is thus a condition of freedom, permitting separation of public and private spheres. Systems like ancient Greek *polis* are political arenas with broader and more subtle exercise of virtue (uncodified know-how), but the price to pay is far less freedom to pursue other activities independently of political control. More predictability in government corresponds to a greater freedom of the other spheres of social life (Larmore [1987, 41]).

2. Equality and Political Liberalism

2.1 Political Liberalism and Rational Dialogue

Charles Larmore's political liberalism doesn't find its justification on a comprehensive conception of good: he rejects what he calls *"political espressivism"*, which "demands that our highest political ideal be mirrored in our highest personal ideal" [1987, 76]. In other words, a liberal doesn't demand that her own comprehensive conception of the good shall shape the basic political principles, which, instead, shall be shared by all citizens: everyone endorsing her own comprehensive moral conception and agreeing on a unique political conception, that is neutral to each other conception. If the ground is "common", we may suppose there is no disagreement on it, and without the existence of a disagreement there is no room for neutrality[39]; for this reason Rawls states that the idea of neutrality is likely to be misunderstood, while the concept of "a common ground" seems more appropriate. In fact Rawls doesn't approach directly neutrality[40] as a justification for his political liberalism, which is

---

[39] See Montefiore's semantic analysis in *Neutrality and Impartiality* [1975].

[40] In *Political Liberalism* Rawls distinguishes neutrality "in terms of the aims" from procedural neutrality [1993, V, §5, 192 and following]. A neutral procedure could entail mere principles of free and rational discussion, but, according to Rawls, this is not enough: such procedure shall be neutral with regard to different comprehensive doctrines and their aims ("their associated conceptions of the good"), but shall not be neutral to the political doctrine: on the contrary, liberalism tends to form and implement political doctrines and to push to comply social behaviours. In this sense, neutrality is not merely procedural but implies certain moral values which constitute the common ground, basis of the political doctrine. Parties in disagreement, during a public decision, choose to set aside their own individual conception (when it collides with others), recognizing that such public morality, shared by the whole society, shall prevail. As Larmore says, liberalism implies a

represented instead by the common ground (overlapping consensus) shared by comprehensive doctrines. But even if a common ground is necessary in order to set up a shared agreement, it's not necessarily given ex-ante. Neutrality has a reason to be for cases in which we must *seek* a common ground: the idea of neutrality intuitively explains the fact that we abstract from our own comprehensive conceptions (putting aside our less binding beliefs) in order to achieve an agreement and a shared (ex-post) political conception. This is the fundamental reason why neutrality should be at the very core of political liberalism, contrary to what Rawls thought.

Larmore specifies that liberalism is seen like "art of separation", opposed to the idea of society as an "organic whole" [1987, 76]. In order to explain what is meant by "art of separation", Larmore introduces the concept of *modus vivendi*, which – he said – implies a divergence "between *citoyen* and *homme*, between 'public' (political) and 'private' (nonpolitical)" [75]. Rawls, in *Political liberalism*, gives a clear explanation of the Latin expression *modus vivendi*: it is used to describe treaties negotiated by States, which are likely to collide. Their reciprocal bargain assures that the signed agreement represents an equilibrium point, so that neither party would have convenience in violating it[41]. According to Rawls, if conditions changed, each party would be ready to pursue its own interest at the expense of the other ones. This means that social balance is virtually unstable. Rawls gives an alternative – and stable – solution: the overlapping consensus among different comprehensive doctrines. He lists the doctrines subject of this consensus [1993, IV, §3, 145]: they

---

separation between "man and citizen" and the political doctrine prevails on the other moral claims ("the right on the good" - or better, on the contentious ideals of good).

[41] In this case neutrality can be considered as the equilibrium outcome of a game among rational players who pursue their own interest. The outcome of the game is affected by mere rational calculus, not moral considerations.

correspond almost to all of those present in our society: all the "reasonable doctrines", with the exception of fanaticism or violent forms of racism[42]. According to Rawls, these doctrines have the peculiarity to be pluralist or to admit a principle of tolerance. People supporting these doctrines accept that "political values normally outweigh whatever nonpolitical values conflict with them" [1993, IV, §3, 146]; therefore, they suit Larmore's perspective of liberalism as "art of separation". But what Rawls emphasizes most is that putting aside conflicting values is an "internal" disposition of the doctrine itself, not just the resolution of a coexistence problem with other doctrines. For instance, a Christian has not a pluralist perspective and would strongly condemn atheists, but her comprehensive doctrine may lead to a principle of tolerance and non-coercion, so that she would demonstrate respect for free choices of people who do not think the same. Thus, the Christian and the atheist would share a stable rule: they can freely express their point of view even if Christian population could easily overwhelm hypothetical few atheists. Rawls, referring to Larmore's theory, expressely rejects the notion of *modus vivendi*, because liberalism is a moral perspective and doesn't consist just in a prudential equilibrium among forces in conflict. Later, Larmore states that what he meant in *Patterns of Moral Complexity* by *modus vivendi* doesn't correspond with Rawls' definition, instead it is a moral conception exactly like the overlapping consensus: the difference with Rawls is "merely terminological" [1996, 133, n16].

If neutrality doesn't rely on "prudential" reasons, it still remains unexplained why should citizens support a neutral way to solve conflicts, instead of imposing their ideas by force: the Christian ideal of toleration, or the simple desire for civil peace, though compatible with many conceptions of good life, seem to represent just partial or shallow explanations, not binding upon

---

[42] It is Larmore who explains that fanaticism or violent racism are examples of non-reasonable doctrines [1987, 60].

all comprehensive conceptions. Minorities could be simply oppressed or random choices could be established (as in a lottery) among different conceptions of good life, bringing to non-neutral decisions. Liberalism over the history found different justifications for neutrality, summarized by Ackerman [1980] and recalled by Larmore in *Patterns of Moral Complexity* [1987, 51] as follows:

- Scepticism (Voltaire, in the *Treatise on Toleration*, 1763): since we cannot find a motivation to justify a certain ideal, no government should try to establish one particular ideal.

- Experimentation (Mill in *Utilitarianism. On liberty. Representative Government*, 1859): each one must be able to try different kinds of life and then exclude the ones bringing less satisfaction. Such experimentation would be hindered if the government would propose to favour only some ideals.

- Individual autonomy (Mill, Kant): everyone must be able to think out by himself her own ideals. According to Lamore this ideal of the person is perfectly synthesized by Fichte (1973) in youth, when he still felt Kantian influence: "No one becomes cultivated, rather everyone has to cultivate *himself*. All merely passive behaviour is the exact opposite of culture; education occurs through selfactivity"[43].

Though these justifications of neutrality may be persuasive to some people, they are all forms of "political expressivism", since in contrast with *modus vivendi* they require our highest political ideal to be reflected in our highest personal ideal (assuming scepticism or experimentation as personal ideals). For this reason they cannot represent a "neutral justification of neutrality" towards different comprehensive doctrine. For

---

[43] See in *Patterns of Moral Complexity* the paragraph *Kantian Liberalism* [1987, 82].

example, people who rejects the universality of scepticism, autonomy or experimentation, or who do not recognize the philosophical arguments sustaining them, probably wouldn't support neutrality of government. Moreover, an experimental spirit leads people to experiment various forms of good life, which may induce a hostile attitude towards religious orthodoxies that claim believers follow certain habits from infancy until the end of life.

According to Larmore [1987, 50-53] a "neutral justification of political neutrality" requires to put aside our own beliefs that the other rejects, in order to "*abstract* from what is in dispute". This justification is based on the universal norm of "rational dialogue". When two people disagree, they may still wish to "solve a more general aspect of the problem", like achieving an agreement about a procedure which can solve the problem at hand, if properly followed. In this case, in order to carry on the conversation it is necessary (see Larmore [1987, 50]):

1. to construct an argument on the basis of her other beliefs that will convince the other of the truth of the disputed belief, or

2. to shift to another aspect of the problem, where the possibilities of agreement seem greater.

This norm is universal (and therefore neutral) because of the definition of rationality and dialogue: without this norm, in case of disagreement, it would be impossible to talk about a disputed topic aiming to reach a solution, or an agreement, either in a rational way (identifying the premise and using logical tools in order to reach the conclusion) and jointly maintaining the *dialogical* dimension of the discussion. To maintain a dialogical dimension means not only to assert what we believe, but also to seek – doesn't matter if it wouldn't be found – mutual understanding. Just to provide an example, suppose two persons disagree about the extent to which redistribution of goods towards the poor class should be implemented. According to the libertarian, no redistribution can be implemented because it consists in an infringement of property rights, but the egalitarian does not believe in property rights as absolutes. He therefore states that rights are important only to the extent that they bring economic efficiency and actual liberty in choosing among different lifestyles, tasks achievable only by means of redistribution. The libertarian may construct an argument on the basis of egalitarian's beliefs, explaining why at the very core of the principle of equality lies the idea of property rights. In turn, the egalitarian explains why property rights are conceivable only if people are considered as equal, but they cannot be equal if redistribution does not redress current balance of power. The problem is that the egalitarian and the libertarian may not agree on the same conception of equality: their different views of the world affect the meaning they attribute to the term "equality". If this was the only problem, it would be easily remedied. In fact, according to Habermas [1973] there is only one "ideal speech situation" that any rational agent would accept, so that each part facing disagreement, through an indefinitely long learning process, would ultimately agree on the same notion of ideal speech: it would be the only one suitable for arriving at the truth. Therefore, if the parts kept on debating, it would be simply a matter of time until they ultimately agree on a certain notion of equality. The problem is that disagreement may be rooted more deeply, on a more abstract level. In fact if the two persons maintain their own vision of the world, they may disagree even on the conception itself of ideal rational conversation, which depends on historical, empirical and linguistic circumstances. Larmore in fact disagrees with Habermas, affirming a contextualist model of ideal justification, independent from the notion of truth. Back to our example, suppose the egalitarian agrees on Habermas' notion of ideal speech. One of Habermas' rules is that "everyone is allowed to question any assertion whatever"[44]. Now suppose the libertarian does not accept that the idea of property rights as absolutes can be questioned (exactly like in a theological discussion within the Church the existence of God isn't questionable): in this case the two persons cannot share a unique notion of ideal conversation. Despite this facts, according to Larmore, the concept of ideally rational conversations "contains some invariants" [1987, 59] that everyone accepts. These invariants are exactly the rules mentioned above: "when disagreement arises, those wishing to continue the conversation should withdraw to neutral ground, in order either to resolve the dispute or, if that cannot be done rationally, to bypass it". Following this rule, the libertarian may offer arguments against redistribution declaring that it may discourage incentives and worsen the condition of the poor class in the long period. In turn, the egalitarian may try to convince the other part not insisting on equality issues, but emphasizing that what is to be redistributed was already part of the properties of the poor class (unjustly subtracted), then redistribution is just a matter of rectification of injustices in the transfer of entitlements. At the end of the process, if they still disagree, they may shift to another aspect of the problem, for example trying to explain why the political costs for the reform may be too high and may cause an unstable situation, such that other more important reforms may be hindered. Or they may agree on a different solution, establishing a voting procedure and letting the majority of voters decide if redistribution should be implemented or not. What is important is that both sides avoid the use of force or deceit and try to offer arguments with intellectual honesty. Their purpose shall be to persuade the other part and achieve mutual understanding, rather than simply persuading an audience so as to obtain a greater number of votes.

---

[44] See *Discourse Ethics: Notes on a Program of Philosophical Justification* in Habermas [1990, 43-115].

2.2   Equal respect and Reasonableness

The norm of rational dialogue only shows *how* to carry on a rational conversation, while it cannot explain *why* to start the dialogue nor *why* to keep on debating when facing disagreement. The underlying motivation is constituted by the moral principle of equal respect. In order to explain what actually equal respect consists in, it is first necessary to distinguish it from other kinds of *respect*. It is not meant as *respect* towards some beliefs: some beliefs deserve it, others not. On the contrary, it has to be considered as *respect* towards persons: it consists in recognizing that, from the point of view of someone else, her own beliefs are justifiable. In other words, equal respect is an attitude involving recognition of the capacity, that everyone possesses, for working out a coherent view of the world. When a person demands that we justify our own action to her, she is recognizing that we have a perspective on the world in which that action makes sense. This implies that if that person indicates her willingness to discuss in a rational way with us, then we have the (moral) *obligation* to treat her as she is treating us. The fact that she has an own moral perspective on the world is the reason for discussing the merits of our action rationally with her (see Larmore [1987, 64]). A principle of reciprocity stands: we respect others (conceiving they have their own moral) if, given our willingness to discuss rationally with them, they show their disposition to discuss rationally with us.

It represents a normative statement, that is not morally neutral towards all doctrines in modern society, but *almost* all. It's hard (though not impossible) that people of modern era could find valid reasons – from their own moral perspective – to reject equal respect. All doctrines endorsing the idea of equal respect can be defined as "reasonable" doctrines. An ought-statement hides behind Larmore's viewpoint: "you must be reasonable", which means you must recognize equal respect as a fundamental moral principle. This could be even considered a definition of reasonableness suitable to Rawls' perspective, as will be explained later[45]. This doesn't imply that any reasonable person would declare to believe in equal respect, if asked. Rather it implies that any reasonable person reading or somehow facing Larmore's theory of equal respect – and understanding it – wouldn't find any reason (from her own perspective) to reject it. If she explicitly rejects it, we can consider that person unreasonable, but the test of reasonableness apply only after a person has become fully aware of the principle. Our assumption is that most of citizens of modern western democracies would stand this sort of "reasonableness test". In fact equal respect is a principle rooted in our democratic culture: public discussion and public justification are at the core of democratic procedures, and they necessarily require this principle. Self-interested politicians may disregard equal respect, but they probably wouldn't admit it in public[46], nor they would consider their own behaviour as moral, if asked themselves.

Justification of equal respect is not fact-dependent, since it is just a normative principle and its appeal belongs to the world of values, it's not a positive truth connected to facts. But if a person believes values depend on facts, the first chapter might be of help to her in explaining why we should endorse the principle. The historical roots of equal respect, the heterogeneity of morality and the genesis of the concepts of tolerance, neutrality and pluralism, do not necessarily represent a justification for it, but they might be, for who believes normative principles are fact-dependent. There are arguments that might persuade us to believe in the norm of equal respect – the first chapter aims to do this – but there are no better arguments than the enunciation

---

[45] John Rawls didn't provide a clear explanation of what reasonableness is, but we can apply the idea of equal respect even to his *Theory*, as will be explained in §2.5.

[46] Politicians are very unlikely to admit to participate in a public debate without being intellectual honest. The notion of intellectual honesty in political discussions might be considered as a result of equal respect.

itself of the principle, since you simply believe in it, or you don't. We are not able to find justifications for equal respect because it represents the very gist of everyone's morality. As Larmore says, we are not required to "justify to ourselves an existing belief except where we have discovered a reason for thinking that by our own lights it may be false" [1996, 150]. Of course, criticisms to the ideal of equal respect have been raised by authors like Seglow, Barry or Sandel, but it will be explained that even if they partially grasp some relevant points, they are not sufficient to threaten the general validity of the principle.

According to Jonathan Seglow, there seem to be two possible forms of justification of equal respect to which Larmore might have recourse: "strong justification" requires that we justify to others our position on terms that they accept as well as us, while "weak justification" requires that we justify to others our position on our own terms, employing beliefs and values which we hold but others may not. In this last case, we sincerely believe that other people are unreasonable not to see matters on our own terms (cf Seglow [2003, 90]). Therefore according to "weak justification" the idea of reasonableness is arbitrarily defined on the basis of our own conception of the good, and those who do not endorse this conception must comply with principles of political association they do not accept. Then rational dialogue is likely to end either in deadlock or oppression of one side by another. This means that "weak justification" do not prevent us from viewing others merely as means to our own ends, and if Seaglow is true, Larmore's liberalism would be a mere affirmation of the superiority of his conception. Even Brian Barry interprets equal respect in the weak sense:

> *"It is perfectly consistent with everything that Larmore says about equal respect that we should believe that the explanation required is an explanation of the superiority of our conception of the good. If we are convinced that nobody could reasonably reject our explanation, we would seem to have done all that 'equal respect'*

can demand of us"
Brian Barry [1995, 176]

It is true that Larmore's theory relies on "weak justification", since reasonableness can be ultimately seen as a notion shaped by a conception of the good. The point is that this conception of the good is so limited to a small set of values (which Larmore and Rawls define as "political values") that it is far more uncontested than the comprehensive conceptions (scepticism, experimentalism or autonomy) or other earlier justifications of liberal neutrality. Nonetheless, Seglow also denies this Larmore's claim, stating that equal respect actually requires the comprehensive conception of autonomy. In fact equal respect demands to treat others as ends, not merely as means, and to recognize the general capacity of persons to adopt ends and values. According to Seglow [2003, 90-91], without the requirement of autonomy, persons could not perceive each other as ends. He underlines how it is possible that a majority of religious believers may institute a state religion satisfying the principle of equal respect: they respect the non-religious minority by simply explaining to its members why they are wrong. The majority would justify its position employing beliefs and values which believers hold but the non-religious minority do not accept (in line with the "weak justification" of equal respect). But according to Larmore a liberal State incorporating religious values into the political morality is inconsistent with equal respect [1989, 581]: the need to abstract from contested beliefs implies that believers shall give up their claims. Seglow replies that this is not a neutral justification, since it forces a division between persons and their ends, making appeal to the partisan value of autonomy. However, his remark is not accurate. It is true that both equal respect and the ideal of autonomy recognize the capacity that everyone possesses for working out a coherent view of the world. Despite this, the fact of having the moral obligation to discuss rationally with who is willing to discuss with us has nothing to do with the fact that everyone has to "cultivate himself", rather than "becoming cultivated", or the fact that everyone ought to have a will unconditioned by empirical ends, as Kantian ideal of autonomy requires. One may grow up through a passive behaviour in education, without autonomous self-activity and merely accepting the rules and conceptions given by the community, and at the same time she may acknowledge the principle of equal respect. Individuals shall not be autonomous, in the sense of being in some way detached or emancipated from the values given by the community, in order to recognize equal respect. Yet, Seglow's criticism is important because it highlights the similarities between political liberalism based on reasonableness or equal respect, and liberalism as a comprehensive conception based on the ideal of autonomy. Nonetheless, Rawls underlines that they present great differences in both scope and generality, and they remain two distinctive and independent conceptions:

> "*The liberalism of Kant and Mill may lead to requirements designed to foster the values of autonomy and individuality as ideals to govern much if not all of life. But political liberalism has a different aim and requires far less. It will ask that children's education include such things as knowledge of their constitutional and civic rights so that, for example, they know that liberty of conscience exists in their society and that apostasy is not a legal crime, all this to insure that their continued membership when they come of age is not based simply on ignorance of their basic rights or fear of punishment for offenses that do not exists [...] justice as fairness does not seek to cultivate the distinctive virtues and values of the liberalisms of autonomy and individuality, or indeed any other comprehensive doctrine. For in that case it ceases to be a form of political liberalism*"
> John Rawls [1993, V, 6.3-6.4, 199-200]

In practice, political liberalism requires citizens to understand "the political conception", then a publicly funded system shall be established. This may imply, in effect (though not in intention), to educate them to a comprehensive liberal conception. Nonetheless, political liberalism honors, as far as it can, the claims of those who wish to withdraw from the modern world in accordance with the injunctions of their religion, although there are unavoidable consequences of citizens' education to a political conception that have to be accepted, often with regret. After all, as Berlin has long maintained, there is no social world without loss (cf Rawls [1993, V, 6.2, 197]).

2.3   The ambiguity of Rawls' *Theory*

It has been exposed the theory of Charles Larmore as equivalent to John Rawls' political liberalism, but the identity between the the two authors' perspectives is not obvious at all. Therefore, before to proceed with the analysis of the concept of equal respect, it is necessary to make it clear why it has been assumed the two authors share the same notion of liberalism. Charles Larmore in *Patterns of Moral Complexity* observes that John Rawls' *A Theory of Justice* presents an element of ambiguity: the presence of an espressivistic conception of liberalism and, at the same time, the idea of *modus vivendi*.

> "A Theory of Justice *(as well as some of Rawls's later writings)* is not all of one piece. Its liberalism contains both modus vivendi and expressivist strands. It is not surprising, therefore, that contemporary antiliberals have homed in on the more vulnerable expressivist components of this book"
> Charles Larmore [1987, p. 121]

This is also the reason why *A Theory of Justice* missed a very clear formulation of some concepts, such as the question of how the primary goods are determined in a neutral way with respect to the conceptions of the good. The element of neutrality was partly hidden under the "veil" of Rawls's personal comprehensive doctrine. So even a central element like the difference principle risked to be interpreted erroneously. But Rawls himself recognizes full knowledge of flaws of his theory, and in *Political liberalism* replies to the criticisms of Larmore:

> *"The distinction between a comprehensive doctrine and a political conception is unfortunately absent from* Theory *and while I believe nearly all the structure and substantive content of justice as fairness (including goodness as rationality) goes over unchanged into that conception as a political one, the understanding of the view as a whole is significantly shifted. Charles Larmore in his* Patterns of Moral Complexity *[…] is quite correct in vigorously criticizing the ambiguity of* Theory *on this fundamental matter"*
> John Rawls [1993, V, §2, n3, 177]

In *The Autonomy of Morality* [2008, 150-152] Larmore further clarifies what constitutes Rawls' ambiguities: it's not clear if he is willing to admit that we must acknowledge a moral authority higher than the political principles we give ourselves, that are merely legitimated by our collective will as citizens (through the original position). In other words, it's not clear if Rawls recognizes the role of equal respect (a moral requirement external to the collective will of citizens) as pillar of his theory of justice, antecedent to the original position. In *Theory* Rawls says that the notion of respect is not "a suitable basis for arriving at" liberal principles of justice [1971, §87, 586]; its meaning must instead be fixed by the principles of justice defined by the original position. This means that the original position defines the notion of respect, not vice versa. Nevertheless, parties in the original position are not merely rational, engaged in the efficient pursuit of their ends, since the conditions on their choice reflect a moral commitment, a sort of readiness to seek fair principle of cooperation: in *A Theory of Justice* the idea of a well-ordered society, in *Political Liberalism* the "reasonableness". The two ideas are very close to each other, in fact there is a continuity between the two books, and the key to properly understand Rawls' theory of justice as fairness is the idea of equal respect proposed by Larmore. The overlapping consensus among reasonable doctrines appeals to a notion of agreement that is not simply actual assent, since the "reasonable" assent is an idealization with normative implications. In fact Rawls' notion of the reasonable is given "by the two aspects of persons' being reasonable [...]: their willingness to propose and abide by fair terms of social cooperation among equals and their recognition of and willingness to accept the consequences of the burdens of judgment" (Rawls [1993, III, §1.2, 94]). Therefore, as Larmore declares, it "has a moral content that effectively implies the principle of respect", and "nothing in this conclusion departs from Rawls' own deepest commitments" [2008, 152]. In this perspective, the features of the original position, like the fact that the parties must think themselves as involved in the construction of a well-ordered society, must rely on moral requirements, given by a principle independent from the collective will of citizens. Parties in original position shall be reasonable, or alternatively, shall endorse the principle of equal respect, even if Rawls didn't expressly acknowledge it. In this sense, equal respect is a pre-condition of the original position and the social contract. Dworkin agrees with Larmore on the fact that "some theory of equality [...] is necessary to explain why the original position is a useful device – or one among a number of useful devices – for considering what justice is [...] The device of an original position [...] cannot plausibly be taken as the starting point for political philosophy" [2000, 118]. Once clarified the ambiguity of *Theory*, in *Political liberalism* the liberal perspective of Rawls seems virtually identical to Larmore's theory. Rawls directly underlines the similarity between his theory of political liberalism and the one of Larmore:

> "I do not know of any liberal writers of an earlier generation who
> have clearly put forward the doctrine of political liberalism. Yet it
> is not a novel doctrine. Two contemporaries who share with me this

general view, if not all its part, and who developed it entirely independently, are Charles Larmore - see for example his "Political Liberalism", Political Theory, XVIII, 3 (August 1990); and the late Judith Shklar - see her "The liberalism of Fear" [...]. It is a great puzzle to me why political liberalism was not worked out much earlier: it seems such a natural way to present the idea of liberalism, given the fact of reasonable pluralism in political life. Does it have deep faults which preceding writers may have found in which I have not and these led them to dismiss it?"

John Rawls [1995, 133, n1]

2.4   The Practice of Equal Respect

As it has been exposed, Jonathan Seglow expressed doubts about the distinction between equal respect and the ideal of autonomy. But he was well aware Larmore clearly denied that political liberalism is justified by autonomy. Then he tried to figure out another form of justification for political liberalism that he calls "empirical neutrality". He is wrong in thinking that liberalism needs any other justification but the principle of equal respect, but his remarks are still interesting because they raise an issue of practical application of the principle of neutrality. Seglow thinks equal respect requires the ideal of autonomy, hence it is not a viable neutral justification of neutrality. Therefore we shall seek a viable justification elsewhere, without falling into the mere affirmation of the superiority of our own conception. The solution can be found in Larmore's "principle of higher neutrality", which Seglow calls "empirical neutrality": it aims at introducing "just as much substantive material into rational dialogue as is needed as a base for making decisions on political principles" (Seglow [2003, 91]). In fact Larmore admits that there are practical limits to neutrality: full neutrality in a modern society may prove too empty to generate any substantive political principles that in some cases shall be necessarily established. When full neutrality makes decisions impossible, then "one should institute only the least abridgment of neutrality necessary for making a decision possible". The "least abridgment" consist in two dimensions (the first dimension is the more neutral):

> "*1. One could admit beliefs that are the least central to anyone's idea of the good life, or*
> *2. One could admit beliefs that the least number of people do not hold*"
> Charles Larmore [1987, 68]

In the second case, neutrality resolves simply in the democratic rule of majority. However it is clear that majority decisions might result in oppression of minorities (tyranny of the majority), which is not justified by equal respect. As Fishkin noted [1989, 156], it could also legitimize the establishment of a state religion if the number of non-believers was relatively small[47]. In the first case instead it would be necessary that each person exhibits a division between central and peripheral preferences: this raises other practical problems, in particular because "centrality" of preferences is fluid and unstable. For instance, prohibitionists might get the censorship of pornographic materials because they hold the central conviction that pornography is an evil, ranked over the non-central preference of consumers to view it. Nonetheless, if the debate was brought back to a matter of principles, the censorship of pornography would be seen as a threat to individual freedom, thus becoming absolutely central even for non-prohibitionists. Therefore also an "empirical principle" of neutrality is undetermined, when applied to a practical problem. As a solution Seglow proposes to reinvisage Larmore's ideal of equal respect in a new way, called

---

[47] This topic will be further analysed in the next paragraph.

"democratic respect". The common ground, or moral consensus, is the aim of rational dialogue, not the pre-requisite:

> *"With public reasons there are no conversational filter or higher principles barring what citizens are permitted to enter into political debate. The only stipulation is that citizens express their proposals in terms that the other side has reason to accept, given a motivation by all sides to do the same. This condition of reciprocity requires that, in seeking to construct shared principles, each side couches its arguments in terms that the other side may accept, even where this may involve revising a conception of the good"*
> Jonathan Seglow [2003, 94]

According to Seglow this version of democratic respect is less demanding than the strong view of equal respect, which requires that parties bracket their conceptions of the good as a condition of their entry into collective deliberations. It is called "democratic" for its tendency to produce in participants an openness to considerations of the public interest: the common ground is the good of a democratic association of equal and free citizens, committed in mutual exchange of public reasons.

Frankly it's not clear why Seglow thinks Larmore's rational dialogue would require to bracket the conception of the good of citizens. The "art of separation" expresses the idea that a liberal doesn't demand her controversial comprehensive conception of good determine the structure of the State, but in rational dialogue conceptions of the good shall be bracketed only when parties face insurmountable disagreement. This doesn't imply they cannot offer reasons in public justification from their own point of view, if in this way they are able to persuade the counterparts. If there is no need of conversational filter in order to keep on debating, they do not have to be applied. Then Seglow's proposal is already implicit in Larmore's equal respect and adds nothing new to his vision. It is perfectly consistent with Larmore's perspective the fact that parties, when facing disagreement, review their conception of the good; yet, this is a success in the practice of rational dialogue.

> *"the norm of rational conversation would serve to shape a political culture in which the public could continue to discuss disputed views about the good life with the hope of expanding the scope of agreement, but in which it would also agree that the state's decision cannot be justified by an appeal to the intrinsic superiority of any such view that remains disputed [...] to believe that we have good reasons for our claim implies the belief that in an ideally rational conversation we could vindicate our claim to others, and to put forward our claim to others [...] is to assert, in effect, that these good reasons should demand the assent of others"*
> Charles Larmore [1987, 54-55].

What is more interesting is Seglow's emphasis on the public interest and the bonds between liberalism and democracy, which is also reflected in Larmore's theory. In fact, in order to justify neutrality it is not necessary just equal respect, but also the fact of feeling themselves as a people, a nation, or a community, which aims to achieve shared political principles (Larmore [1996, 142-144]). The willingness to justify our perspective to others is not enough, the rational dialogue applies only to people who are already interested in devising principles of political association. In fact if people living together are not interested in reaching a coexistence agreement, they wouldn't even start a debate on this problem. The pursuit of shared political principles is the pursuit of a "common ground", but the feature itself of being committed to pursue a common ground is a "common desire" that may be seen itself as a "common ground". This is precisely the public interest Seglow's democratic respect requires. We have to be placed under peculiar conditions such that we think ourselves like engaged in a common enterprise, for example if we share historical experience and memory of past conflicts, even civil war, that were sparked by opposing ideals but now give way to a shared practice of equal respect (see Larmore [1996, 143]). Or else, common language, geographic position and, more generally, a spontaneous interest for the good of a democratic association. Resembling an expression of John Locke, Larmore calls this sort of common feeling an *original Compact,* that must precede the contract [1996, 143]. The theory of political liberalism and equal respect are worth within precise boundaries of modern western societies, that we also may see as democratic associations. Larmore never made secrets of the strict bond between equal respect and democracy.

> *"equal respect is precisely what makes democratic self-rule the proper form of political association. Citizens can therefore understand themselves as the source of law only insofar as they have already accepted this principle and judge the validity of their collective decisions from this standpoint"*
> Charles Larmore [1996, 221].

These considerations are also useful in order to counter argue the most important criticism moved to political liberalism by Michael Sandel.

2.5   The Romantic Critique of Individualism

In *Patterns of Moral Complexity* Larmore deals with communitarian criticisms to moved to John Rawls' *A Theory of Justice* by Sandel, in *Liberalism and the Limits of Justice* [1982] and in *The Procedural Republic and the Unencumbered Self* [1984]. His concern lies with the weaknesses of the Kantian form of justification (the ideal of autonomy) that, he argues, dominates Rawls' work. The ideal of the person as unencumbered by natural and social circumstances, and so prior to its ends and values, is unacceptable to Sandel. He states that Rawlsian ideal of priority of the right over the good is justifiable only if we believe that "the person has an empirically unconditioned sense of duty"[48], like the ideal of autonomy requires. In this perspective the person is erroneously conceived as disembedded from her purposes, because we actually have constitutive attachments to particular visions of the good life, which are not valuable because we freely choose them (as Kant thought), but for they are "inseparable from understanding ourselves as the particular persons we are". Divested of our own purposes, we lack "moral depth", therefore we cannot attribute to the "disencumbered self" a capacity for moral responsibility. In other words, the ideal of autonomy ignores the inter-subjective constitution of the self within the community. It is at the very core of individualistic philosophical outlook (thrived during the Enlightnment) and challenged by the so-called Romantic critique, nourished by the ideals of tradition and sense of belonging. The self, without purposes and sense of moral responsibility, cannot choose moral principles like Rawlsian principles of justice. This is the paradox of the disembedded self, purified of all those features dependent on natural and social circumstance (as the veil of ignorance requires), but at the same time situated in a particular circumstance, because committed to the achievement of the social agreement (in the original position). Further, Sandel observes that the circumstances of justice, namely the conditions set by the conception of a well-ordered society (assumed by the parties in original position), are inconsistent with the priority of the right. In fact since they are empirical circumstances, they cannot be unconditionally valid, independently from our particular conceptions of the good and social (empirical) environment. This last Sandel's observation is a mistake, because his objection turns on the fallacy that if something is "empirical"

---

[48] A simple example of empirically unconditioned duty is, for instance, the sense of duty prescribing that we must tell the truth, even if in a particular circumstance to tell the truth may imply evil (under certain aspects) consequences. A duty of this kind is purely deontological, disregarding any consequentialist reasoning.

there is some serious possibility it could be different. On the contrary, "relative material scarcity, limited altruism and conflicting conceptions of the good life are, however empirical, also universal features of the human condition"[49] (Larmore [1987, 126]). Moreover, Larmore says that Sandel cannot demonstrates Rawlsian principles lack an adequate foundation, because the neutral attitude the parties adopt in the original position can be justified by equal respect, rather than by the ideal of autonomy. In fact "*A Theory of Justice* harbors, side by side, the Kantian and the modus vivendi approach" (Larmore [1987, 125]. This is precisely the ambiguity of Rawls's *Theory*. In conclusion, Rawlsian liberal theory does not require that a controversial conception of the good be mirrored in the political order, as the espressivist ideal of autonomy does.

However, Sandel is right to say that Kantian ideal of autonomy cannot justify liberalism, because an espressivist model of political theory cannot justify neutrality, since it is not unanimously accepted, as communitarian critique highlights. On the other hand, even Sandel endorses an espressivist model of the political order, since he "seems to prefer the fantasy that society as a whole once was or might become a family or a club of friends [...] this point is historically irrelevant, since nonliberal societies, past and present, have scarcely been an idyll of fellow-feeling" (Larmore [1987, 126]). Fantasy or not, what really matters is that this organicist conception of society is controversial and Sandel is wrong in assuming that we must choose between Kantianism and some form of communitarianism, that are two forms of political espressivism. On the contrary, neutrality justified by equal respect can be the fundamental principle shared by both communitarians and rawlsian liberals. In fact, as it has been exposed in paragraph 2.3, we can interpret Rawls' idea of reasonable as the acknowledgement of the principle of equal respect as antecedent

---

[49] These are all conditions of Rawls' well-ordered society.

to the original position (which is best understood as a position of neutrality, therefore comparable to the procedure of rational dialogue (cf Larmore [1987, 44]) then antecedent and requisite of the political principles that parties establish. This form of political liberalism is morally rooted within the bonds of the community we belong. Equal respect is a broadly shared ideal among people belonging to modern western societies, and is shaped by our common culture and history, as explained in the first chapter. Though it prescribes a neutral procedure of deliberation (the rational dialogue), equal respect is a moral concept that is not built (or invented) in a constructivistic way. To put it in a way dear to Walzer: the relevance of equal respect could be acknowledged embarking the path of moral interpretation, not moral invention (see §1.5).

Despite equal respect is a normative principle, Larmore provides a sort of factual (or descriptive) statements as justification for his neutrality: "we are almost all reasonable", which is a sort of "almost" universal standard. He seems to believe that in practice, in empirical application, no sufficient objections (no large number of supporters, nor strong ideas) would counter his principles (neutrality and equal respect) so much that they could be jeopardized. Despite this claim, Larmore is aware that his justification of liberal theory is not cosmopolitan, but "situated" in an empirical context. In regions and societies with a different history, where pluralism, tolerance or the political form of nation-state are unknown ideals, the only appeal to reason cannot justify equal respect. It is only in the history of western world that rational dialogue and equal respect are general and shared principles (even by critics of autonomy and individualism). Equal respect has not the attribute of truth as absolute, rather it carves out its empirical context, since it represents Larmore's answer to the long-debated question among liberals and communitarians: the Romantic critique of modern individualism. The goal of political liberalism is just to refute the claim "that liberalism makes sense only as affirmation of individualistic views about the good life". It "seeks to detach the principle of political neutrality from the fate of this view" and it does not represent a force "that work against the Romantic values of belonging and tradition" (Larmore [1996, 151]).

Larmore raises the question of how to justify equal respect to those who do not believe in it. Actually – he states – there's no need to justify a belief to those who are not interested to discuss with us about it, namely those who bring no equal respect. A liberal political system needs not to feel obliged to reason with extremists, intolerants or fanatics, "it must simply take the necessary precautions to guard against them" [1987, 60]. However, we might also seek a justification valid for ourselves, but "we cannot see how to justify it, because it defines the framework of what we understand moral argument to be" [1996, 150]. In fact we haven't yet discovered a reason for thinking that by our own lights equal respect may be false. This doesn't mean we may discover it in future. In fact, it might happen that "modern experience is to dissolve in the light of the one irresistible, all-encompassing Good" [1996, 151][50]. In this hypothetical scenario, political liberalism would be no more the solution for a theory of justice in political philosophy, but only another part of the problem.

Even if Larmore proved liberalism is a conception independent from the ideal of autonomy, there's a last communitarian objection:

---

[50] Think of the case scientific progress brings new lights about an ultimate theory of everything, linking together all the physical aspects of the universe, which would have dramatic implications on our way of thinking of metaphysics and our conception of political philosophy. The same can happen for cataclysms, a nuclear war (indeed, if humanity is on the brink of extinction our view of political order would be likely to change), the coming of a new messiah or an alien descent.

> *"Present-day communitarians, of course, have called attention on the distinctive common life necessary for political association and have argued that it must embody substantive visions of the good and feelings of belonging that go beyond the formal principle of equal respect"*
> Charles Larmore [1996, 143]

According to Larmore in this remark there is a grain of truth, but communitarians didn't brought into focus. In fact it's true that it is necessary a sort of sense of belonging preceding the social contract, but it doesn't involve conflicting conceptions of the good. Instead, it is represented by the above mentioned *original Compact* (see §2.4). Anyway, Larmore says that there exist forces that imperil the vitality of historical memory, threatening in this way the tightness of the *original Compact*. Against this threat, he concedes that liberal polities must keep alive a sense of the past experience from which they derive [1996, 144]. It therefore seems that in a liberal State the role of education shall be covered (at least partially) by public institutions. This is in line with Rawlsian argument about children's education discussed at the end of paragraph 2.2.

Up to this point, it seems Larmore has overcome all challenges moved to liberalism. Nonetheless, there is a further criticism Sandel raised [1989] which cannot successfully objected by liberals. In fact the principle of equal respect – even when acknowledged – is not considered of utmost importance by everyone. There are other values that may have priority in some persons moral, for example the value of human life. It would result in the "life principle", which we may refer to as the principle holding that everyone has right to live and no one has the right to take her life (maybe with the exception of some consequentialists reasons, in case we have to secure lives of others). It may conflict with equal respect in cases like the discussion about the right of abortion. If we considered the fetus as a person, abortion would indeed represent an infringement of this principle (except the case mother's life is in danger). Then if abortion is considered as bad as killing a child, how much moral weight equal respect can bear? Many persons would probably feel themselves morally entitled to impose their conviction by law on others, disregarding the principle in order to defend the right to life, of greatest importance. As Nagel puts it:

> *"After all, liberal equality is only one value, however important, and there will inevitably be others too powerful for it to contain. If someone is really convinced on religious grounds that abortion is as bad as killing a child, the requirement of equal respect for his fellow citizens may be incapable of persuading him that he should refrain from imposing that conviction by law on others who do not share it"*
>
> Thomas Nagel [2006 b]

Moreover, Sandel [2006] thinks it is not possible to decide about the question of abortion without taking a stand, implicitly or explicitly, on the moral status of the fetus: liberals would do better to engage their opponents on the moral merits, rather than retreat to an unconvincing neutral ground. In Sandel's view [1989, 135], bracketing our moral substantive beliefs is impossible. In fact, after having bracketed our beliefs, we still are not able to find a solution. If we leave the question be decided by the will of people, liberalism resolves in the simple rule of majority, which leaves room for the "tyranny of majority". If on the contrary we think individual women should decide, we prevent majorities to impose their values, but we are affirming in this way an "autonomous conception of the person such as the voluntarist view" (Sandel [1989, 136]).

Sandel's arguments are valid, but limited to very few cases, which do not imply political liberalism is morally untenable. The validity of his arguments is even narrower than what we may expect. First, as Nagel says, there are even "Catholics who defend the legal right to abortion while holding that abortion is morally wrong" [2006 b], but this would be only a contingent justification of equal respect. If equal respect owes its validity to the life principle, its validity would be contingent upon some other considerations, like our notion of the foetus, and not as absolute. What is significant is that there are even reasons for thinking that equal respect has intrinsic validity, completely independent from the life principle. In fact in societies with death penalty, when we execute someone we shall provide her a justification. One may believe to be morally entitled to execute an outlaw, because of her serious crimes, but without such a justification she would never bring the outlaw to the gallows pole! In this case the principle of equal respect is considered prior to the life principle. In other cases, if it wouldn't be possible to provide reasons to the victim (because there is no time, or because that person doesn't speak the same language, as during war is likely to happen), the executioner would provide at least to herself a moral explanation for her action. To provide reasons for our actions, either to ourselves or to others, is at the core of morality. It may happen we do not provide any justification at the moment, and in this case we are more likely to do evil things[51], but if put in front of our conscience, we will probably seek reasons and try to explain why we acted in good or evil way. To *give reasons* is of utmost importance: morality requires us to act in accordance to what we perceive as reasons. Likewise, public justification requires us to provide reasons for our actions. This second statement, closer to the definition of equal respect, is therefore strictly tied to what we consider morality itself.

Since our willingness to discuss rationally is the way we practice equal respect when facing disagreement, and given the centrality of equal respect in morality, Sandel makes a critical mistake in not recognizing the centrality of freedom of speech. As Nagel underlines, Sandel "might accept a fairly strict rule protecting political speech because it would be too time consuming to

---

[51] Often, evil may be simply a function of thoughtlessness, as Hannah Arendt thought [1968]

decide in every case whether it was on balance beneficial or harmful. But he seems to think that if there are limits on censorship they have no more fundamental justification than that" [2006 a, 45]. Instead, freedom of expression do not owes its validity on whether it serves valuable ends, but has intrinsic value connected to equal respect. It might be extended even to Nazi demonstrators, provided that they are not violent. If a person is genuinely convinced that a certain race or group of people is inferior under certain aspects, the right way to deal with racism is to counter argue her arguments involving her in rational dialogue, rather than censoring her ideas. Rawls in the paragraph *Toleration of the Intolerant* [1971 §35, 219] says that the liberties of the intolerant may also persuade them to a belief in freedom: "this persuasion works on the psychological principle that those whose liberties are protected by and who benefit from a just constitution will [...] acquire an allegiance to it over a period of time" and will tend to lose its intolerance and accept liberty of conscience. These are good reasons that might have been raised in defending the right to march of the Nationalist Socialist Party of America, which held the march in Chicago in 1978[52]. However, this doesn't mean freedom of speech is purely a deontological principle and do not admit exceptions. In fact if the intolerant sect rises so strong initially that it can impose its will straightway, or does grow so rapidly that the "psychological principle" has no time to take hold, then its freedom should be restricted. It should happen only "when the tolerant sincerely

---

[52] Federal Judge Bernard M. Decker expressed in this way the principle in striking down the Skokie ordinances which initially prohibited the march: "It is better to allow those who preach racial hatred to expend their venom in rhetoric rather than to be panicked into embarking on the dangerous course of permitting the government to decide what its citizens may say and hear [...] The ability of American society to tolerate the advocacy of even hateful doctrines [...] is perhaps the best protection we have against the establishment of any Nazi-type regime in this country" (Illinois Issues 13, November 1978)

and with reason believe that their own security and that of the institutions of liberty are in danger" (Rawls [1971 §35, 220]). Apart from Nazis or intolerants, what is important is that freedom doesn't depend on whether it serves valuable ends. Any kind of censorship implicitly bears a particular conception of the good, which the liberal State shouldn't endorse. Otherwise the risk would be too high, represented by some sort of totalitarian ethic or any softer version of it. Isaiah Berlin remarkably dealt with this issue:

> *"The possibility of a final solution – even if we forget the terrible sense that these words acquired in Hitler's day – turns out to be an illusion; and a very dangerous one. For if one really believes that such a solution is possible, then surely no cost would be too high to obtain it: to make mankind just and happy and creative and harmonious for ever – what could be too high a price to pay for that? [...] Since I know the only true path to the ultimate solution of the problem of society, I know which way to drive the human caravan; and since you are ignorant of what I know, you cannot be allowed to have liberty of choice even within the narrowest limits, if the goal is to be reached"*
> Isaiah Berlin [1998, 15-16]

2.6   Equality of Welfare

This second chapter offered a brief summary of the philosophical premise founding political liberalism, profiting by the keen analysis of Charles Larmore. Different motivations lead to the acceptance of the principle of neutrality instead of imposing by force our own perspective: they can be merely prudential (entailing just self-interested rational calculus), or involving different moral arguments: scepticism, experimentation, the liberal value of autonomy, or the desire of civil peace. Not mentioned yet, even the fact of being sympathetic[53] with the situation of other persons may be a good argument, since it encourages ourselves to abstract from our own interests, or beliefs, in order to reach an agreement with them. But none of these arguments is sufficient and all-encompassing: political neutrality needs a neutral justification, and this can be found in rational dialogue, that is merely procedural and is undertaken only when an *original Compact* already exists. The rational dialogue is morally supported by the principle of equal respect, that is an "almost universal" normative principle, explaining why we should start to dialogue. Equal respect is a principle broadly shared among people belonging to the modern western society, since it is shaped by our common culture and history. For this reason, political liberalism is a conception morally rooted within the bonds of the community we belong. Equal respect can also be considered at the very core of Rawls' theory of justice as fairness, representing its ultimate justification. But one may ask if the principle does have also implications in the economic world. Charles Larmore intends equal respect in a "rather minimalist sense", since "other senses are too substantive, for example [...] egalitarianism, which require equal distribution of certain basic resources or equality of opportunity" [1987, 61]. Other authors have a different opinion, like Ronald Dworkin who thinks equal respect has more substantive implications. This and the next paragraph investigate this issue[54].

Dworkin distinguishes various conceptions of equality in order to decide which of the possible schemes may represent an

---

[53] Sympathy is different from respect [Larmore 1987, 62-63]: "Sympathizing with another's belief consists in believing that in his situation it would have been our own, so we can broaden our sympathy to the extent we can imagine sharing another's perspective".

[54] Here is presented and revised Dworkin's theory proposed in *Sovereign Virtue: the Theory and Practice of Equality* [2000]. The first two chapter of the book, object of this analysis, were already published in Dworkin's *Philosophy and Public Affairs* in 1981

attractive political ideal. The first concept is "equality of welfare" (distinguished from equality of resources), which holds that treating people as equals means to distribute or tranfer resources among them until no further transfer would leave them more equal in welfare [2000, 12]. The practical application of this ideal is very problematic, because welfare is a concept depending on enjoyment, satisfaction or success, missing a clear definition and being sensitive to alterations. For example it is very hard to find a univocal measure of satisfaction, and persons disagree even on what it means to be successful. One person might prefer to be a lousy artist to being a brilliant lawyer, because she thinks art so much more important than anything lawyers do. Then she might either think her life as artist is successful simply because she is an artist, or think that she can achieve success only being brilliant in her job and therefore undertaking the career of lawyer.

If equality in welfare means equality in success, two persons are supposed to be equal if they both have fulfilled their preferences. But preferences may be both personal and impersonal, the last concerning the world in which we live, included the political system. If a person prefer a socialist system hardly could be fulfilled as much as a person who prefers a capitalist system, if society has to decide between these two systems or a few other viable alternatives. There are even political preference adverse to equality of success which indeed cannot be fulfilled by this concept of equality: a racist outlook may imply that blacks shouldn't have as much power or success as whites. On the other hand, personal notions of success are not less problematic. In fact people perceive success and failure in very different ways. One may consider her life of a busy peasant who achieves very little and leaves nothing behind as full of value, while another person thinks that such a life is only full of failure (cf Dworkin [2000, 36]), but at the same time she is not even satisfied by her comfortable life of office worker. It wouldn't seem to be fair a

State redistribution towards the last person in order to achieve the equality of success.

Another paradoxical situation occurs in the case of "expensive tastes" [2000, 48]: "equality of welfare seems to recommend that those with champagne tastes, who need more income simply to achieve the same level of welfare as those with less expensive tastes, should have more income on that account". Furthermore, the measure of satisfaction, enjoyment or success could be either established by the person herself, or by what is supposed she would have established in case she had been access to perfect information. It makes the difference since persons often judge their success relatively to their potentiality or ambitions and considering what they would have ideally achieved if they were more lucky, more talented, more rich. For example one may feel dissatisfied since she believes she could have been a famous actor, given her talent and beautiful aspect. In this case she would receive transfers by the government in order to reach equal welfare. Of course her subjective considerations may be wrong and would merely represent an opinion, rather than a real satisfaction. If she knew (under perfect information) she is not actually so beautiful and talented compared to others, she maybe wouldn't consider her life so unsuccessful and then she wouldn't be entitled to the transfers. The fact that the State should intervene in distributing resources for this purposes would be very controversial, even if it was actually possible to reach a certain ideal of equality of welfare. A person's own judgement, even if fully informed of the facts, will reflect her own philosophical convictions or tastes about what gives value to life and this wouldn't be objective [2000, 32] nor necessarily "reasonable" (in a broad sense). We might try to let persons make comparative judgement, each using her own standard between what is her actual life and what could have been her ideal life, and then comparing these comparative judgements, in some way that they neutralize their philosophical convictions.

Even if this comparison had sense for two persons (and this is really unlikely), it would be impracticable for the entire society indeed.

Neither theories of "objective welfare" are more promising. They may assume that people are wrong in what they take to be important, or even in what they would take to be important if fully informed about pertinent facts [2000, 45]. But in this case the political system requires officials who relies on their own judgements about what gives value to life in redistributing wealth. If friendship was considered an objective source of satisfaction by the officials, but a person do not recognize it, the government could be entitled to spend resources in order to educate that person, with the purpose of making her satisfied, such that she learns how to appreciate that value. Transfer of money or resources could even not be helpful in increasing the welfare of a certain person. If a person is convinced she deserves a certain social position she cannot have without removing another one from that position, it couldn't be possible to satisfy one without reducing the welfare of the other below the hypothetical threshold of equality.

One last paradoxical case to consider is the condition of people with mental or physical disabilities. In many cases those with handicaps have in consequence less income [2000, 60], and then do not have equal material resources with others. But this doesn't imply they have lower levels of welfare. As Dworkin underlines, Tiny Tim is happier than Scrooge[55], but we wouldn't think Scrooge entitled to extra resources (as equal welfare requires) while Tiny Tim has neither enough money to afford physiotherapy. Another odd situation is expressed by the example of the "paraplegic violinist". The paraplegic can lead a more normal life thanks to a machine the community can provide to him, levying a special tax. But she prefers to purchase a superb Stradivarius with the same funds: her welfare might be

---

[55] They are characters of Dickens' novel *A Christmas Carol*

in fact increased more by owning the violin than by having the machine. But in this case other violin-lovers would have reasons to complain, since they can affirm to have as much claim to use extra funds as the paraplegic has if funds are spent in this way [2000, 62].

Dworkin analysis is far more subtle and detailed, considering much more particular cases and even combining them in different views of equality of welfare. However nothing more needs to be said, since it is obvious that this conception of equality is far from being responsive to the moral requirements of the principle of equal respect exposed in the preceding paragraphs of this chapter. Since it is even too difficult to imagine how could such a scheme work in theory, in practice it would probably produce catastrophic consequences. It is also completely inefficient from an economic point of view and leaves room for frauds and deceit. For example, a person might "cultivate expensive tastes in order to steal a march on others, so that it would reward improper efforts if she were to receive more income" and then secretly spend that income in other goods, thus gaining more enjoyment others can afford [2000, 50]. In conclusion, the ideal of equality of welfare is untenable from all points of view.

2.7   Equality of Resources and Free Market

The conception of equality favoured by Dworkin is "equality of resources": it holds that treating people as equals means to distribute or tranfer resources among them until no further transfer would leave their shares of the total resources more equal. Political philosophers and ordinary citizens often picture equality as the antagonist or victim of the values of efficiency and liberty supposedly served by the market. On the contrary, Dworkin tries to suggests that the idea of an economic market "as a device for setting prices for a vast variety of goods and services, must be at the center of any attractive theoretical development of equality of resources" [2000, 66]. He constructs a simple artificial exercise to illustrate this point: a number of shipwreck survivors are washed up on a desert island and any likely rescue is many years away. They accept the principle that no one is antecedently entitled to any of the resources abundant on the island, but they shall instead divided equally among them. For simplicity, Dworkin supposes they do not think it might be wise to keep some resources in common and resources can physically divided into *n* identical bundles. At least provisionally, immigrants also accept the following "envy test" of an equal division of resources: "no division is equal if, once the division is complete, any immigrant would prefer someone else's bundle of resources to his own bundle" [2000, 67]. At this point, if the identical bundles were distributed, the envy test would be met, but there are other reasons that may hinder the fairness of the distribution and fail to satisfy the immigrants. In fact many immigrants might like all the resources included in their bundles, while others might hate plover's eggs, abundant in each bundle. They do not prefer other bundles, since they are all equal, but they would have preferred other treatment of the initially available resources, combining them differently so that different bundles were composed. One may argue that trades after the initial distribution might improve persons' position, but the others might have no reasons to trade their bundle and therefore trade would be unlikely to result in the ideal bundle for everyone. The immigrant supposed to be elected to achieve the division of resources needs another device to compose the bundles which avoid arbitrariness and unfairness of distribution, meeting at the same time the envy test. The solution is a sort of market procedure: the auction [2000, 68]. The divider hands each immigrants an equal number of clamshells in themselves valued by no one, to use as counters. Each distinct item on the island is listed and the auction determines its price. At the end of the auction no one will envy another's set of purchases because, by hypothesis, she could have purchased that bundle with her clamshells instead of her own bundle. Moreover, each person played an equal role in determining the set of bundles actually chosen. No one find himself with resources she doesn't care.

In a community that has dynamic economy with labor, investment and trade, once the auction is completed, if immigrant are left to produce and trade as they wish, the envy test will shortly fail. Some may like to work harder, producing more, others may be more skilful, others may fall sick or a lightning may strike their farm. We must ask "whether (or rather how far) such developments are consistent with equality of resources" (Dworkin [2000, 73]). First suppose all immigrants are equal in talents, but they hold different tastes and ambitions. If one wants to work harder in order to reach her ambitions, she might achieve a higher social position or might accumulate more wealth than others. She could be envied by others, but only if we look for envy at a particular point in time. Instead, envy should be seen as a matter of resources over an entire life, and a person's occupation is a part of the bundle of the goods. We must apply the envy test "diachronically" [2000, 85]. In fact a certain person may enrich because she assesses the value of her time dedicated to leisure lesser than the value perceived by the fruits of her hard work. If others preferred to have more free time, they cannot claim for a redistribution from the richer, hard worker, in the name of the envy test over lifetime. Moreover, one may assess the value of a certain good in the initial auction, let's say a plot of land, precisely in virtue of how she thinks she can exploit the land in future. Her assessment, even if she didn't finally purchase the plot of land, contributed to determine the final price of that land in the auction and therefore even the relative prices of all other resources in society. Value of resources is then determined not by their intrinsic value, instead is measured in terms of what persons' decisions "cost others" [2000, 84]. For example, if Bruce wants to buy the land in order to build a tennis court, he has to reckon with Adrian's choice of producing tomatoes on the same land. At the end of the auction, Bruce might get the land, but its cost doesn't depend only on what Bruce or other competitors in the auction think they will be able to earn from the tennis court, but depends even on Adrian's opportunity-cost to earn from the sale of tomatoes produced on the same land. In fact, tastes and desires of consumers determine the demand for tomatoes, which in turn affects the cost of the tennis court, partly contributing to determine the cost (price) of playing tennis, and in the same way, the relative prices of all the resources. Breaking the chain at whatever point would invalidate the initial auction, advantaging or disadvantaging particular conception of the good life. In other terms, "people should pay the price of the life they have decided to lead, measured in what others give up in order that they can do so" [2000, 74]. If tomatoes were more demanded by consumers, in the auction Adrian would bid a higher price for the land and if Bruce wanted to buy it anyway, he would have to pay more. If community redistributed resources, like part of the land or the tomatoes produced by the land, or if someone claimed to fix the price of those tomatoes, it would be unfair (as well as inefficient, as economists point out), since it would mean to influence or hinder persons' choice of life (in this way violating neutrality and equal respect) while provoking distortions in the entire system of pricing: the initial auction wouldn't have determined the same initial bundles if immigrants had known that community would have brought into play redistribution. As Dworkin affirms, it seems that "the initial auction would produce continuing equality of resources even though bank-account wealth became more and more unequal as years passed" [2000, 85]. Therefore the market "is endorsed by the concept of equality, as the best means of enforcing, at least up to a point, the fundamental requirement that only an equal share of social resources be devoted to the lives of each of its members, as measured by the opportunity cost of such resources to others (Dworkin [2000, 112]).

However, people do not have the same talents nor the same luck, and this may have implications on the concept of equality of resources. Considering first the impact of luck on the immigrants' post-auction fortunes, Dworkin distinguish between two kinds of luck:

> *"Option luck is a matter of how deliberate and calculated gambles turn out – whether someone gains or loses through accepting an isolated risk he or she should have anticipated and might have declined. Brute luck is a matter of how risks fall out that are not in that sense deliberate gambles. If I buy a stock on the exchange that rises, then my option luck is good. If I am hit by a falling meteorite whose course could not have been predicted, then my bad luck is brute"*
> Ronald Dworkin [2000, 73]

Differences between optional or brute luck may be a matter of degree, for example if someone develops cancer have brute luck, but if she smoked heavily in the course of her life it may be considered optional luck. The solution in dealing with luck is the insurance. People taking out the insurance are risk-averse, others are more risk-prone. Since the insurance has a cost (the premium), they pay the price of the life they have decided to lead, and a safer life (chosen by risk-averse people) is more costly. Those who take out insurance and never activate it, or those in bad luck who are not insured, cannot claim to be compensated. This can be explained considering the following argument: at the initial auction, immigrant could purchase lottery tickets with their clamshells, but what they paid for them (some amount of other resources) will be wholly forgone if the ticket does not win. There shouldn't be redistribution between those who gamble and win and those who lose, because, as Dworkin explains, "redistribution would make some forms of life less attractive or even impossible" [75, 2000]. Nonetheless, for the case of brute lack there are some exceptions to the general rule: the uninsurable brutal lack. For example, if someone is blind from birth, it's clear that she cannot take out insurance against blindness, since no one can buy insurance after the event. Moreover, it may even happen that one is more likely to become blind due to her genetic, therefore she is inclined to buy more coverage than others, but this wouldn't reflect a difference in opinion about the value of different forms of life, more or less safe. She could even be discriminated by the insurance provider, forced to pay a higher premium, given her genetic propensity to disease. Not everyone has an equal risk of suffering some catastrophe that would leave her handicapped. For these cases, equality of resources requires to compensate them through a fund collected by taxation or other compulsory process (Dworkin [2000, 77-78]). Dworkin expresses this mechanism bringing the story of the immigrants up to date:

> "By way of supplement to the auction, they now establish a hypothetical insurance market that they effectuate through compulsory insurance at a fixed premium for everyone on the basis of speculations about what the average immigrant would have purchased by way of insurance had antecedent risk of various handicaps been equal"
> Ronald Dworkin [2000, 80]

At this point the question raises if it would be fair to treat as handicaps some eccentric or expensive tastes and preferences. At a first glance the answer seems negative, but this issue is more subtle than expected if we considered someone who finds she has a craving (obsession, lust, or in the words of psychology a "drive") that she wishes she did not have, which causes frustration or even pain. In certain cases homosexuality may be considered within this framework, to the extent that certain homosexuals declare they would be better-off without it.

However, the difference with other kinds of unwanted preferences seems too subtle and opaque. What matters according to Dworkin is that it seems very unlikely that many people would purchase an insurance against the risk of particular tastes [2000, 82] or sexual orientations. For this reason this case couldn't be compared to the example of people with handicaps. A different matter is represented by those tastes closer to what we commonly perceive as disease, for example the case of paedophilia[56].

The last and most critical issue is whether talents are a valid reason for intervention in the market, as uninsurable brutal luck is. Dworkin answer is affirmative to this question, but the solution he proposes is irremediably catastrophic. The problem Dworkin deals with is the trade-off between ambitions and talents: we must allow the distribution of resources to be ambition-sensitive, that is, "to reflect the cost or benefit to others of the choices people make"; but on the other hand we must not allow the distribution of resources to be endowment-sensitive, that is, "to be affected by difference in ability of the sort that produce income differences in a laissez-faire economy among people with the same ambitions" (Dworkin [2000, 89]). We might look to an income tax that neutralize the effects of differential talents, yet preserving one person's choosing occupation and ambitions. But we cannot hope to define, even in perfect information, a tax that identifies only the component of wealth that is traceable to differential talents as distinguished from differential ambitions. Talents in fact are nurtured and developed, and ambitions and talents exercise reciprocal influence on each other, as Dworkin acknowledge [2000, 91]. Moreover, a tax cannot discriminate among individuals with different personal situation. Therefore Dworkin solution is the "underemployment insurance": an insurance against the

---

[56] Dworkin doesn't explicitly mention the cases of homosexuality and paedophilia.

probability of earning lower income due to a lack of talent. There is no actual insurance market against lack of what we ordinarily take to be skill, as there is against catastrophes that result in handicap, nevertheless Dworkin try to imagine a hypothetical market in this way:

> *"suppose that before the initial auction has begun, information about the tastes, ambitions, talents, and attitudes toward risk of each of the immigrants, as well as information about the raw materials and technology available, is delivered to a computer. It then predicts not only the result of the auction but also the projected income structure – the number of people earning each level of income – that will follow the auction once production and trade begin"*
>
> Ronald Dworkin [2000, 94]

To collect all this information is not only impossible in practice, but also highly problematic (if not impossible) in theory. Besides, whatever result would be probably extremely fluid and unstable. Anyway, according to Dworkin the insurance would protect people against not having the very highest income projected for the economy by the elaboration of the computer. The computer would be able to establish (at least roughly) the difference between how much a person actually earn and the income they would have if endowed with the highest level possible of ability (talent). The chances of winning would be extremely high, "since very few immigrants will turn out to have the maximum earning power" and therefore "the cost of the premium will be extremely high as well" [2000, 96]. This implies that the insurance would be probably a bad bargain for the policyholders. Therefore Dworkin underlines how it is necessary to lower the income level chosen at the covered risk: in this case the policyholder who lacks of talents and does not have a successful career would get a lower amount as insurance reimbursement, but in exchange the premium is far more accessible. Being the premium lower, the penalty for who is able to get the maximum earning is lower as well [2000, 98]. At this point we might translate the insurance structure in a public scheme, where the premium is represented by a compulsory tax.

This scheme of insurance has serious problems both theoretical and practical, some of them already mentioned, other depending on considerations about moral hazard and administrative costs. For example, Dworkin is aware that "both the incidence and the amount of payments from the fund depend on what the recipient could earn if willing", then some people may cheat by hiding their abilities [2000, 100]. But even honest people cannot know what they might earn at a given occupation without trying (any try may imply half a lifetime of preparation). A test to discover latent talent would be necessary, and it would be extremely costly. The burden of proof might be assigned to policyholder in order to reduce moral hazard, in this case they have to demonstrate their attempt and efforts in achieving a certain objective and at the same time their lack of talents. In any case the cost of accuracy in determining people's actual abilities to earn would be too high and the goodness of the result too uncertain. Dworkin is aware of the many limits of his model: "We might decide that a tax scheme so closely modeled on this hypothetical insurance market is offensive to privacy, or too expensive in administrative costs, or too inefficient in other ways". He concludes that "a scheme that ties redistribution to actual earnings rather than to ability to earn", might be a better second-best approximation [2000, 102].

Actually, Dworkin underestimates the difficulties in distinguishing between effort or ambitions and talents, while overestimates the capacities and possibilities of a "central planner". To put in place this insurance mechanism would mean to concede officials or politicians the arbitrary power to decide about likely controversial notion of "effort", "ambition" and "talent", which imply the power to hinder or favour some conceptions of the good life. Probably the inefficacy of the insurance scheme – publicly funded – combined with very high administrative costs, would produce serious distortion in the pricing system and the free market structure that Dworkin convincingly advocated until this moment. The fact that no actual market insurance of this sort ever existed is the clearest indicator of how much it is unrealistic and unfeasible.

However, a more fundamental criticism has to be moved against this kind of insurance, which attacks upon the motivations that would have led Dworkin to elaborate his model. The justification of the insurance scheme is the envy test, but what exactly people envy those who had success? If they envy their talent, it is something they can never achieve, since no one can transfer talents from a person to another (at least not by taxation or income redistribution). Indeed, a person may develop a particular talent thanks to a certain amount of resources, in this way redistribution may help. But a transfer towards the insured aims at improving their opportunity to develop talents, that is not what exactly they envy, since we assumed they desire the talent itself, not the opportunity. Moreover, many of those gaining reimbursement won't probably spend it in developing their talents. However, people may envy the wealth or welfare of a successful person instead her talent. But in this case it is not clear why their envy should be legitimate. In fact, as it has been exposed, not any kind of envy is legitimate according to the conception of equal resources (for example not the envy "at a particular point in time") and wealth per se shouldn't imply consequences liable to be redressed by means of public redistribution. Even actual welfare of those we think of as successful people might be only a superficial impression: they may be depressed, they may feel anxious precisely because of their social position, they may have family problems or they may have serious or embarrassing problems in sexual relationships. The same applies if envy is connected to a sort of indignation against inequalities, since inequalities per se have no moral implication, to the extent that the initial auction may produce continuing equality of resources even though bank-account wealth became more and more unequal. If instead people envy the opportunity a successful person had in the course of her life, then it's not clear why the transfer aimed at neutralizing differences in income should be considered a better solution with respect to other welfare programs based on education, training courses, reintegration into the labor market and so on.

Dworkin didn't take into account the extremely discouraging psychological mechanism that his insurance scheme could produce. In fact if it was actually practicable in a market economy, those who would take out the insurance were already implicitly endorsing the idea that they are likely to fail in getting the desired job or achieving the desired social position (which by hypothesis they desire, otherwise they wouldn't envy the person earning the maximum income and they wouldn't even take out insurance). This means that they are convinced in advanced to have no talents or to have high chances to have no talents, nor they imagine the possibility that they could be able to successfully shape their talents thanks to hard commitment and ambition. Self-esteem and motivation may be fundamental for the development of talents and this "loser" psychological approach could lead to ruinous economic disincentives. If a person asks the public administration for an help "ex post", admitting she can't achieve the desired objective, we can imagine she at least had a try, with hard work and real dedication, in reaching her objective. Instead, if a person is disposed to take out an insurance of this kind "ex ante", then she is probably thinking to relax, or cheat, in any case giving up hope and ambitions. This kind of person would be probably the only one to insure if a market insurance of this sort would be practicable, and similarly would be the only one glad to pay the tax for the insurance premium if it was included in a welfare state program.

A simpler and less problematic version of equality of opportunity will be exposed in the next chapter, relative to Rawls' principles of justice and in particular the difference principle. But before, one final consideration has to be made about the conception of equality of resources. Our starting point was an artificial exercise where shipwreck survivors, deprived of any kind of good, were washed up on an island starting off equal in resources. Nonetheless, in actual societies people do not "start" in the same fair circumstances and there are theories about inheritance taxes and initial acquisition of property rights that are much debated and challenged by many fronts. These topics are discussed in the fourth chapter.

3.   The Difference Principle

Charles Larmore rises some doubts about the justifiability of the difference principle: in order to justify it, it is necessary to abandon the idea that the principle expresses our deepest personal ideals (conception that Rawls seems to embrace in *Theory*, instead). Larmore continues:

> *"A more promising approach might be to base the neutrality of this principle on more purely political considerations […]. Everyone agrees that the state must play some role in regulating the distribution of wealth, and so such intervention must be neutral with regard to the interests of rich and poor. Whether this will suffice to ground the difference principle, of course, is a more complex question, involving both normative and economic considerations. My aim is not to answer it here (indeed, it is rightly controversial whether this particular welfarist principle should be upheld, and the answer may be negative). My aim is to indicate how the question should best be discussed"*
>
> Charles Larmore [1987, 129]

It is possible to neutrally justify the difference principle in the perspective of political liberalism, and this is one of the main issues dealt with in this essay. Explaining how to justify John Rawls's principle under a liberal perspective is a necessary premise in order to justify Rawls's political liberalism, since his revisited theory in *Political Liberalism* maintains the same fundamental principles of *A Theory of Justice* almost unchanged. This means that elements already present in *Theory*, like the difference principle and the conception of primary goods, can be understood in a neutral way with respect to comprehensive conceptions of the good life. The interpretation provided in this paper outlines a clearer and lucid vision of Rawls' theory of justice as fairness.

3.1   Inconsistency with the Maximin Rule

The second principle of justice states that "the social and economic inequalities are to be arranged so that they are both (a) reasonably expected to be to everyone's advantage, and (b) attached to positions and offices open to all" (Rawls [1971, §11, 60]). Rawls later specifies [§46, 302] that the point (a) refers to "the greatest benefit of the least-advantaged" (members of the society): this coincides with the difference principle. As Valeria Ottonelli writes in *Leggere Rawls* [2010, 107], this means that "egalitarian measures need to be implemented to the point where any further step in the direction of egalitarian order would be counter-productive, in the sense that would worsen the condition of the lower classes rather than improve it". The affirmation is correct, but the problem is that the limit above which additional measures become counter-productive (for those situated in the worst conditions) would leave a redistribution leeway much smaller than assumed by the interpreters more fascinated (or frightened) by the tension of the egalitarian theory of Rawls. Secondly – and this is the crucial point – the "condition of the lower classes" is understood in complex terms and not as a single dimension (like income or wealth in monetary terms), nor as a single dimension at a time – even in the practical application of the principle! – but is considered "as a whole". Therefore it is necessary to analyse what should be the correct interpretation of the principle of justice.

It is first necessary to distinguish between a "weak" and a "strong" reading of the difference principle[57]. This distinction is

---

[57] This is even Cohen's opinion expressed in *Rescuing Justice and Equality*. He speaks about the "strict" and "lax" readings of the principle, underlining the "ambiguity" of Rawls:

> "...*the difference principle, which endorses all and only those social and economic inequalities that are good for the worst off or, more generously, those inequalities that either make the worst off better off or do not make them worse*

already outlined by Andrea Villani in *Giustizia Distributiva e Scelte Collettive*, who refers to the difference principle writing:

> *"...the strong reading that inequalities (e.g. in the distribution of income) shall be allowed providing that they result in only an aid to disadvantaged, or rather in the weak sense [...] that inequalities are permissible providing that they result <u>also</u> (necessarily, but not only!) in an aid to the disadvantaged, which is radically different"*
> (translation mine)
> Andrea Villani [1988, 204]

Villani explains why he supports the second interpretation, starting from the analysis of the "principle of redress": it would be related with the difference principle because the last "gives a certain weight to the consideration singled out by the principle of redress" (Rawls [1971, §17, 100]. Rawls explains that, according to the principle of redress, "undeserved inequalities call for a redress; and since inequalities of birth and natural endowment are undeserved, these inequalities are to be somehow compensated for" [100]. But in spite of what seems to be derived from the general principle, Rawls argues with an example that "in pursuit of this principle greater resources might be spent on the education of the less rather than the more intelligent, at least over a certain time of life, say the earlier years of school" [100]. The difference principle does not require that natural endowment to be levelled off: it doesn't require that "the society attempts to abolish disability, as if everyone should run

---

off: in this matter there is a certain ambiguity of formulation in Rawls. [...] We confront here two readings of the difference principle: in its strict reading, it counts inequalities as necessary only when they are, strictly, necessary, apart from people's chosen intentions. In its lax reading, it countenances intention-relative necessities as well. So, for example, if an inequality is needed to make the badly off better off but only given that talented producers operate as self-interested market maximizers, then that inequality is endorsed by the lax, but not by the strict, reading of the difference principle. I shall argue that each of these incompatible readings of the principle is nourished by material in Rawls's writings, so that he has in effect two positions on the matter"
Gerald Allan Cohen [2008, 29, 69]

the same race from a fair starting point" [100]. This approach seems very evasive and restrictive compared to the enormous subversive tension of the values inherent in the principle of redress. Nevertheless, Villani insists that strictly speaking also the principle of redress does not seem to bring equality, like Rawls says (in the above mentioned quotation) and also like Mark Plattner thinks: quoting Plattner [1979], Villani concludes that despite the egalitarian premise and the opposition to the merits, the expectation (made explicit) in *Theory* is actually that of a society not much different from the USA present society (Villani [1988, 112]). In the following pages it would be explained why the only possible way to understand the difference principle is through the comprehension of what Villani called "weak reading". On the contrary the "strong reading" isn't compatible with a liberal perspective.

The strong reading can be graphically represented by the maximin utility function. It is also commonly known by economists and reported in textbooks as "Rawlsian social welfare function"[58] (see graph in *Figure 2*), but it's not suitable to explain Rawls's ideas. On the contrary, if used with this purpose, it would be absolutely misleading. If we conceived a conception of justice based on *Figure 2*, we would upset what expressed in *A Theory of Justice*, where the illustration of the difference principle is more complex (see *Figure 3*, §3.3, taken directly from Rawls' *Theory*) and cannot be understood disregarding the following considerations.

First, it is necessary to clarify that Rawls himself points out that the difference principle and the maximin rule are two distinct

---

[58] For example *Scienza delle finanze* by Harvey S. Rosen e Ted Gayer (third Italian edition 2010, ed. Chiara Rapallini) refers to Rawls and the original position, reporting at p. 142: "he also states that in the initial situation the citizens would choose a social welfare function based on the criterion of the maxmin, because this is a kind of insurance against the most disastrous outcomes" (translation mine) and draws a graph similar to that shown in *Figure 2*.

elements and we shouldn't confuse one another: "Despite the formal resemblance between the difference principle as a principle of distributive justice and the maximin rule as a rule of thumb for decisions under uncertainty [...], the reasoning for the difference principle does not rely on this rule. The formal resemblance is misleading" [2001, §27, 94-95]. He further underlines that "the failure to explain this was a serious fault in *Theory*" [2001, §27, 95, n17] and "it is not essential for the parties to use the maximin rule in the original position. It is simply a useful heuristic device. Focusing on the worst outcomes has the advantage of forcing us to consider what our fundamental interests really are when it comes to the design of the basic structure" [§ 28.3, 99]. Various authors mixed up the topic: "the maximin rule was never proposed as the general principle of rational decision in all cases of risk and uncertainty, as some seem to have thought[59]. Again, Rawls highlights that instead of "«the difference principle», many writers prefer the term «the maximin principle» [...] But I still use the term «difference principle» to emphasize first, that this principle and the maximin rule for decision under uncertainty (§28.1) are two very distinct things; and second, that in arguing for the difference principle over other distributive principles [...] there is no appeal at all to the maximin rule" [2001, §13, 43, n3]. All the passages mentioned are extracts from *Justice as fairness*, but they even apply to *A Theory of Justice*; in fact, as Rawls states, the difference principle does not change and the "revisions in the second principle are merely stylistic" (Rawls [2001, § 13.2, 43]).

---

[59] For example, see J.C. Harsanyi, in his review essay, «Can the Maximin Principle Serve as a Basis for Morality?»" (Rawls [2001, §28, 97, n19])

Figure 2: Maximin Utility Function

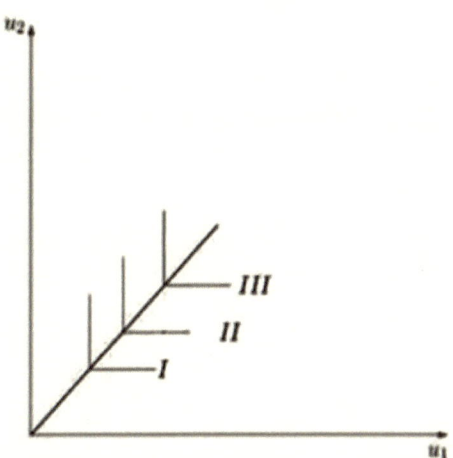

Analysing the graph in *Figure 2*, the incompatibility between the difference principle and the maximin utility function comes easily to light. Assume that u_1 is the utility of the individual who is better, u_2 of the one who is worse off; I, II and III are indifference curves (for the same level of social welfare). If a curve is higher than the other, it expresses a greater social welfare. The distribution of goods in society would determine a point within the quadrant (located on one of the indifference curves of social welfare) which identifies a given utility for the individual corresponding to u_1 and for the one corresponding to u_2. For the present, we assume the hypothesis that what is represented is utility, in general terms. Actually for Rawls is not so, as explained hereinafter, since he doesn't deal with utility, but primary goods. To simplify, we can speak of utility "if we assume utilities to be linear in indexes of primary goods" (Rawls [2001, §62, 62]). Now, according to the chart, it can be noticed that:

    1. if the utility of the worse off individual decreases because of the increasing utility of the better off, the point representing the distribution moves towads a curve located

below. Therefore, to maximize social welfare, it is not possible to increase the utility of an individual if this is at the expense of the individual who is worse off.

2. It is indifferent, in the calculation of social welfare, increasing u_1 if this increase does not correspond to an increase of u_2. This is because the social welfare is equal to the utility of the individual who is worse off.

This seems directly deductible from the second principle of justice, for this reason often equated to the maximin function. But according to Rawls's discussion of the difference principle, for each point listed above we should make an important observation:

1. Rawls assumes that it is not possible (at least "up to a certain point") increasing u_1 (who is better situated) without even u_2 increases.

2. Since it is not possible to increase u_1 without resulting in an increase of u_2, it would never be indifferent increasing u_1, since this increase would always benefit the individual who is worse, at least "up to a certain point"

Rawls's assumption is absolutely fundamental. He states what follows:

> "as we raise the expectations of the more advantaged the situation of the worst off is continuously improved. Each such increase is in the latter's interest, up to a certain point anyway. For the greater expectations of the more favored presumably cover the costs of training and encourage better performance thereby contributing to the general advantage"
> Rawls [1971, §26, 158]

The principle doesn't force to an egalitarian arrangement. Rawls doesn't consider as indifferent (as instead it would result from the maximin) an increasing of u_1 on equal terms of u_2 (who is worse off), which enhances inequality between the two. Rather, he states that, precisely in virtue of the principle, "it must be reasonable for each relevant representative man [...] to prefer his prospects with the inequality to his prospects without it" (Rawls [1971, §11, 64]). The same concept is repeated in *Justice as Fairness*:

> *"This is because over time the greater returns to the more advantaged serve, among other things, to cover the costs of training and education, to mark positions of responsibility and encourage persons to fill them, and to act as incentives [...] plainly the difference principle [...] recognizes the need for inequalities in social and economic organization, of which their role as incentives is but one"*
> John Rawls [2001, §18.2-19.2, 63-68]

These passages are the foremost confirmation of Andrea Villani's idea of weak reading of the principle: "inequalities are permissible providing that they result <u>also</u> (necessarily, but not only!) in an aid to the disadvantaged".

3.2   Long Term Expectations and Contractualist Theory

The reason why increasing utility of the individual who is better off would lead to an improvement of those who are worse off can be more accurately explained as follows. If we had a cake to be shared between two individuals, and we start giving more slices to those who are better off, as a consequence it would remain less available to those who are worse off indeed; but the assumptions behind Rawls' considerations are very different, since the condition of representative[60] individuals must be considered under the following circumstances:

---

[60] *"When principles mention persons [...] the reference is to representative persons [...]. I assume that it is possible to assign an expectation of well-being to representative individuals [...]. This expectation indicates their life prospects as viewed from their social station. [...] neither principle applies to distributions of particular goods to particular individuals who may be identified by their*

1. by means of a reasoning that takes into account the expectations in the long term, not the immediate allocation of resources;

2. in complex terms, through an index of primary goods.

Rawls doesn't deal with utility, but only with expectations. To clarify what he means with the term "expectations", he introduces the concept of primary goods[61]. In *Justice as Fairness* he specifies that "the index of primary goods [which are object of the distribution] is an index of expectations for these goods over the course of a complete life" (Rawls [2001, §51.5, 172]), therefore Rawls' theory doesn't deal with the question of immediate allocation of income at some point in time. In addition, as would be discussed hereinafter, the choice between different distributions of primary goods is restricted to the choice of some different schemes of cooperation. These "schemes of cooperation" may include, for example, anarcho-capitalist systems as well as more regulated welfarist systems. In this sense, to choose the right scheme is a different issue with respect to the choice on how to allocate resources already available. Anyway, it can be demonstrated that, with regard to the distribution, even considering only the mere income rather than an index of primary goods (thing that even Rawls does in some exemplifications), the criterion of maximin is not appropriate to explain the difference principle. The reason is that the legislator (or anyway the one who chooses how to redistribute) must be in the original position to deliberate. The veil of ignorance implies that the "persons in the original position have no information as to which generation they belong. These broader restrictions on knowledge are appropriate in part because questions of social justice arise between

---

proper names"

John Rawls [1971, §11, 64]).

[61] In fact paragraph 15 of *A Theory of Justice* titles "Primary Social Goods as the Basis of Expectations" (Rawls [1971]).

generations as well as within them" (Rawls [1971, §24, 137]). Therefore is sufficient to consider the conditions imposed by the original position to conclude that it's improper to raise an argument concerning only the short term. Instead, it's correct to subsume a variety of topics that go far beyond the pure economic ones, even when the decision concerns the redistribution of income, rather than an index of goods. In fact, the psychology and the motivational law (taken into account under the veil of ignorance, as Rawls himself states [1971, §24, 137-138]) leads to formulate policies far more complex than the immediate monetary (or material) compensation for the disadvantaged. In a broader view, deducting wealth (even just in the monetary sense) from the rich to give to the poor may, in the long run, damage (right in monetary terms) the poor themselves. The ambition, the hopes of reaching a better condition or the benefits of competitive struggle are elements that play a crucial part in this context. Redistribution can increase the utility of those who are worse off (and therefore the social welfare) in the short term, but it could also worsen their situation in a broader context. In this sense, the limit for which more egalitarian measures would be counterproductive becomes much lower than what assumed in "the strong reading" of Rawls's principle of justice. An excessive state aid can lead, over time, to a loss of utility of individuals who are only initially advantaged. Ronald Dworkin says that these are doubtful propositions, but they represent a popular argument among libertarians:

> "Many economists believe that reducing economic inequality through redistribution is damaging to the general economy and, in the long run, self-defeating. Welfare programs, it is said, are inflationary, and the tax system necessary to support them depresses incentive and therefore production. The economy, it is claimed, can be restimulated only by reducing taxes and adopting other programs that will, in the short run, produce high unemployment and otherwise cause special damage to those already

at the bottom of the economy"
Ronald Dworkin [1985, 209]

In this regard, as Rawls says: "I shall not consider how far these things are true. The point is that something of this kind must be argued if these inequalities are to be just by the difference principle" [1971, §13, 78]. For these reasons, *Figure 2* is not pertinent in order to consistently explain the difference principle. Rawls raises an entirely different issue, for which the criterion of maximin is totally inadequate:

> *"the difference principle is not intended to apply to such abstract possibilities. As I have said, the problem of social justice is not that of allocating ad libitum various amounts of something, whether it be money, or property, or whatever, among even individuals. Nor is there some substance of which expectations are made that can be shuffled from one representative man to another in all possible combinations"*
> John Rawls [1971, §26, 157-158]

To allocate *ad libitum* a certain quantity of goods is instead a matter of "allocative justice", while Rawls rises a problem of "distributive justice" (see Rawls [2001, §14]). To allocate resources between individuals with given preferences concerns utilitarianism rather than the contractualist theory of justice as fairness. Villani makes this point clear while referring to Salvatore Veca's analysis of allocative and distributive justice proposed in *Utilitarismo e contrattualismo. Un contrasto tra giustizia allocativa e giustizia distributiva*: "Veca defines utilitarianism as a theory of allocative justice and contractualism a theory of distributive justice [...] The allocative justice subsumes, we can say, an «instantaneous» way of giving resources, concerning individuals (i.e. preferences) with no space for their history, nor the relations between them" (Villani [1988, 235-236], translation mine). Therefore, unlike utilitarianism, which tries to allocate resources or goods between individuals with given preferences and in a particular moment in time, the question posed by the theory of justice as fairness requires instead to evaluate principles regarding a stable cooperation between individuals or groups over time. Dworkin's conception of "equality of resources" is compatible with issues of distributive justice, not allocative justice. In fact we must apply the envy test "diachronically" (Dworkin [2000, 85]) rather than at a certain point in time, as is explained in the previous chapter (§2.7). The "condition of the community", which in case of utilitarianism (or allocative justice), is assumed, in case of contractualism (or distributive justice) is central because it is itself the achievement of social choice (see Salvatore Veca [1986, 114]). The choice on the condition of the community implies a way to weigh individual preferences, that is defining legitimate and illegitimate interests of citizens. This could also suits various utilitarians: in fact, as noted by Villani, all utilitarians but Bentham, including Harsanyi, tended in some way to weigh individual preferences before including them in the "social calculation"[62]. However Villani states [1988, 234] that normally, utilitarians pose no formal criteria to define legitimate and illegitimate interests, and to distinguish between them. Veca puts it in this way:

> *"The contractualist theory proposes, in other words, to answer the question remained open for utilitarianism of preferences of Harsanyi: can you find a criterion of legitimacy about preferences and interests?* [...what matters in contractualist theory] *is not the simple fact that we have preferences, or that we are centres of pleasure or pain and we have goals, but the fact that we are able to reason about preferences that we happen to have, and while doing so, we recognize the others as similar to us, and therefore worthy of equal respect*[63]: *recurring issues of distributive justice are at the core of a contractualist approach"* (translation mine)

---

[62] "calcolo sociale" in the original

[63] It can be excluded Veca refers to Charles Larmore's ideal of equal respect (*Patterns of Moral Complexity* is published afterwards, in 1987), but it is very interesting to note how the basic intuition is exactly the same.

Salvatore Veca [1986, 108, 116-117]

Veca and Villani's analysis are published in the Eighties, before the issue of *Political Liberalism* (1993); hence their reference is only *A Theory of Justice*. Rawls in *Justice as fairness* provides good evidence to confirm what they wrote: "Observe that particular distributions cannot be judged at all a part from the claims (entitlements) of individuals earned by their efforts within the fair system of cooperation from which those distributions result. In contrast to utilitarianism, the concept of allocative justice has no application" [2001, §14.2, 50-51]; and then specifies: "the two principles of justice incorporate the concept of pure background procedural justice and not that of allocative justice" [2001, §51.4, 170-171].

In conclusion, it's possible to say that contractualism lies "upstream" of utilitarianism, namely it rises issues that have priority on the matters posed by utilitarianism and which are very constitutive of the basic patterns of morality (and the basic structure of society). It is first necessary to establish what are the legitimate or illegitimate interests; then only once established the moral foundations of the political order, laid down by the theory of justice as fairness, the issues raised by utilitarianism can be put under consideration or to the vote. Utilitarianism would be considered as one of the various comprehensive conceptions of good, to which the doctrine of political liberalism must remain neutral, ensuring coexistence with other comprehensive conceptions. For example, utilitarians might support a reform to boost the economy, such that the net balance of individual utility is maximised. This might be pursued, providing that it is compatible with the fundamental principles of justice laid down by the contractualist theory of justice as fairness, and that its repercussion doesn't disadvantage a particular conception of good life.

3.3   Complex Terms Condition and Primary Goods

The paragraph above is devoted to the discussion of the first assumption to take into account when dealing with   the difference principle: the fact of considering the expectations in the long term. The second assumption to be analysed is that conditions of individual shall be measured in complex terms, through an index of primary goods. In the theory of justice as fairness, with regard to the problems of distributive justice Rawls makes use of the concept of expectation, rather than utility. The expectations are not composed by the satisfaction that citizens believe they are capable to get through the available goods. If so, the index of primary goods should embrace all persons' conceptions of good. In the previous chapter (§2.6) it has been exposed why a theory of justice cannot properly achieve equality of welfare and why the concept of welfare, success or satisfaction may implicate unsurmountable problems when applied to distributive issues. Instead, primary goods aren't determined on the basis of an amount of satisfaction they yield when employed, so they don't depend on specific conceptions of good, nor they determine conceptions in any way. They are only means that citizens, in the measure they can get them, can use (or not use, if they prefer not to) to pursue their own conception of good. In this way they are compatible with Dworkin's conception of "resources". Primary goods are, in a nutshell, the social values of "liberty and opportunity, income and wealth, and the social bases of self-respect" (Rawls [1971, §11, 62]). So the condition of the least advantaged is meant in complex terms, not about a single dimension (for example only income or properties), and the way inequality can be "redressed" concerns the redistribution of all these social values as a whole. However, it might be objected that in applying the redistribution considering at the same time all dimensions in complex terms (income, self-esteem, fundamental liberties, etc.), there's a risk of reducing Rawls' principles of justice to total indeterminacy. Therefore, while applying the second principle of justice, it might be plausible to distinguish among different dimensions and apply the difference principle within the limits of a single dimension at a time. Sometimes, for practical purposes, it may happen to consider only one dimension at a time, like income, but certainly it's not the case when any objection to proceed in this way is presented. A good argument against an application of the principle calculating only one dimension at a time is suggested by Rawls' analysis presented in *Justice as fairness* (§51: "The flexibility of the index of primary goods"), where Amartya Sen's proposals (exposed in *Choice, Welfare, and Measurement* [1986, 353-356]) are commented by Rawls: "primary goods themselves should not be viewed as the embodiment of advantage, since in fact advantage depends on a relation between persons and goods" [2001, §51, 168]. Here Rawls emphasizes that the index of primary goods he proposes "does not take into account, and does not abstract from, basic capabilities" [2001, §51.2, 169]; on the contrary, it "fully recognizes the fundamental relationship between primary goods and persons' basic capabilities. In fact, the index of those goods is drawn up by asking what things, given the basic capabilities included in the (normative) conception of citizens as free and equal, are required by citizens to maintain their status as free and equal" [2001, §51.2, 169-170], including civil and political liberties and so on. Provided this, if the worth of a good is based on the ability of an individual, and if those capabilities also depend on other goods like liberty or opportunity (as it is intuitive), it would unlikely be completely abstracted from the overall vision of the index of goods and it couldn't be determined considering a dimension at a time. Moreover, considering that the choice of the society is restricted to different feasible schemes of cooperation (as further explained later), it couldn't be granted to a representative individual a combination of primary goods formed by an amount of income and social bases of self-respect defined *ad libitum*. These goods would be closely connected to each other within a certain scheme of cooperation and therefore only certain combinations would be achievable, namely the one given (or feasible) for each scheme. Rawls takes a stand to support these arguments:

> *"Yet it seems extraordinary that the justice of increasing the expectations of the better placed by a billion dollars, say, should turn on whether the prospects of the least favoured increase or decrease by a penny [...] Part of the answer is that the difference principle is not intended to apply to such abstract possibilities. The possibilities which the objection envisages cannot arise in real cases; the feasible set is so restricted that they are excluded. The reason for this is that the two principles are tied together as one conception of justice which applies to the basic structure of society as a whole"*
> Rawls [1971, §26, 157-158]

The two principles are tied together as one conception of justice applying to the basic structure of society as a whole. In fact one last point to underline is that the difference principle cannot be considered independently from the other principles of justice.

> *"It is sometimes objected to the difference principle as a principle of distributive justice that it contains no restrictions on the overall nature of permissible distributions. It is concerned, the objection runs, solely with the least advantaged. But this objection is incorrect: it overlooks the fact that the parts of the two principles of justice are designed to work in tandem and apply as a unit [...] We cannot possibly take the difference principle seriously so long as we think of it by itself, apart from its setting within prior principles"*
> John Rawls [2001, §13.5, 46, n10]

Moreover, the principle of equal liberty in general is already implicitly included in the difference principle, since liberty is one of primary goods. Then the first principle comes into play only when it is necessary to give to liberty an order of priority over other primary goods and "this priority rules out exchanges («trade-off», as economists say) between the basic rights and liberties covered by the first principle and the social and economic advantages regulated by the difference principle" (Rawls [2001, §13.5, 47]). The first principle could simply be a kind of clause of the second, which specifies that, among primary goods, fundamental liberties have a "utility" so great that, whatever combination of goods is obtained, the individual deprived of liberty is considered the one worse off. This particular view of the two principles helps a better comprehension of how the difference principle operates. In fact, thanks to this explanation, it's easier to imagine both Rawls' principles as illustrated in *Figure 3*, and thus to convey a broader outlook over Rawls' theory of justice. The clause, anyway, is relevant since it is not absurd to speak about utility of liberties or other elements of primary goods, like Rawls does: "these liberties are the same for all citizens (are specified in the same way) and the question of how to compensate for a lesser liberty does not arise" [2001, §45.1, 149]. In fact, Rawls distinguishes between the freedom as "equal liberty" and the "worth of liberty"[64] [1971, §32, 204], just as if it couldn't be assigned any worth to "equal liberty". On the contrary, my hypothesis is that, focusing the attention on a single principle of justice (the second, plus the clause derived by the first) the worth of "equal liberty" would simply be so high that it cannot be compared to the "value of liberty" nor the one of other primary goods. Now,

---

[64] In a nutshell, we can say that the concept of equal liberty defines a balanced scheme of fundamental liberties (which are political ones, as it is wider explained in *Justice as fairness* [2001, §45, 148 and following]: to ensure a particular liberty requires to restrict or regulate another, so it is necessary to organize a system of liberties that depends on the totality of limitations they are subjected to. This system is guaranteed as exactly alike for all, according to the first principle. Instead the worth of liberty can vary, for example: the ones who are richer can take more advantage of their own liberty of opportunity, in this sense it has a greater worth. The worth of liberty depends on the index of primary goods and is governed by the difference principle.

it is clear that the *Figure 2* (introduced above and related to the maximin criterion) is not suitable to illustrate the difference principle at all. Therefore, below is shown the illustration of the difference principle as it appears in *A Theory of Justice* (or *Justice as fairness*, where there is only the graph on the right, see *Figure 3*). The path followed in previous paragraphs might have been useful in order to immediately understand the mechanics represented in the graph below. Initially, it was introduced the hypothesis that improving the expectations of the more advantaged, the level of those who are worse off rises continuously. Furthermore, for each relevant representative individual "must be reasonable to prefer his own prospects with the inequality rather than his prospects without it" (Rawls [1971, §11, 64]) and "the difference principle [...] recognizes the need for inequalities" [2001, §19.2, 68]. Therefore, starting from the picture of the criterion of maximin, we have to consider only the part of the figure, consisting in those points (assuming that x_1 is the individual who is better) that are located to the right of the bisector, which corresponds to all points of perfect equality. It makes no sense to consider indifferent that our own condition is placed in whatever point on the curves of social welfare shown by the graph on the left, as implied by the maximin. In fact, we know that increasing utility (meant as a linear function of primary goods) of x_1, then even utility of x_2 improves, thus leading society to a curve of greater social welfare.

Figure 3: The Difference Principle

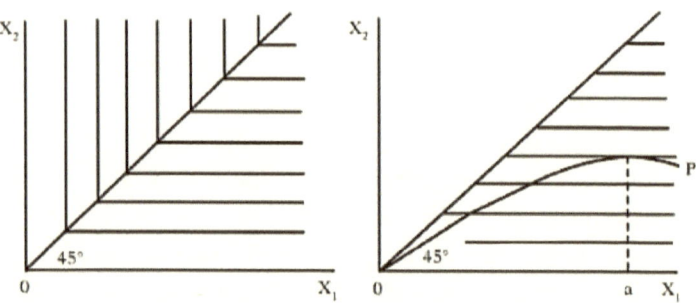

The curve OP (P stands for production) is given for a certain scheme of cooperation. There are different curves OP, more or less efficient, among which the society can choose. For example, we can imagine a libertarian and anarcho-capitalist scheme of social cooperation, or at the opposite a welfarist scheme more inclined to state aid policies, each of them with its own curve OP. The fact that the choice is restricted to different "schemes of social cooperation" (i.e. different OP curves) excludes that it's possible to choose among different allocations *ad libitum*. In fact, even x_1 and x_2 are "specified by reference to their shares in the output and not as particular individuals identifiable independently of the scheme of cooperation" (Rawls [2001, §18, 63]). The problem of distributive justice is precisely to identify which scheme, or curve OP, is more efficient and to reach the higher point "a" on this curve. The term "scheme of cooperation" used by Rawls is rather generic, but we may assume that a curve can vary from one to another simply thanks to the introduction of a legislative reform. In order to choose the best alternative, we know that one "scheme is more effective than another if its OP curve always gives a greater return to the less advantaged for any given return to the more advantaged" (Rawls [2001, §18, 63]). The return, as seen above, can be measured as utility, that is a linear function of the primary goods in complex terms, taking into account that the choice of cooperation excludes those systems which do not guarantee fundamental liberties, according to the priority of the first principle. In other words: utility would fall dramatically if these liberties were not guaranteed, excluding in this way that particular scheme rather than others. It may be that the priority of the first principle does not appear justifiable in certain cases. The first principle about priority of liberty, in fact, can be considered (although Rawls doesn't express the concept in these terms) part of the difference principle, as a clause stating that the utility attributed to fundamental liberties is so high that they are not exchangeable with other primary goods. Under certain conditions, it appears unreasonable and it may prevent the principles of justice from being justified in certain societies, like for example those in which there is an extreme lack of resources, since there it might seem justifiable to exchange some liberties with other primary goods. In fact, in conditions of extreme need in which it is difficult to ensure the survival of individuals, it might appear unfair to prevent someone from the voluntary exchange of some liberties for other primary goods (like food). But it should be noted that Rawls' principles of justice suite only a society which remains in a condition of moderate scarcity. This is an assumption of the whole Rawls's theory: "the circumstances of justice obtain whenever mutually disinterested persons put forward conflicting claims to the division of social advantages under conditions of moderate scarcity. Unless these circumstance existed there would be no occasion for the virtue of justice" [1971, §22, 128]. This is a fundamental point, without which it would be difficult to justify, aiming to an overlapping consensus, the principles of justice, especially the priority of liberty.

In order to choose the fairest scheme, we have to look at which one reaches the highest line among the "equal-justice lines"

(Rawls[2001, §18.1 62]) that are the part of the indifference curves situated at the right of the bisector. When utility of the individual who is better off grows too much, then "even though the index [of primary goods] increases for the more advantaged group [...] the reciprocity implicit in the difference principle no longer obtains" (Rawls [2001, §18.1, 62-63]). As Rawls specifies [§18.1, 62], the alternatives in which the total utility is higher (where is maximized the sum of utilities, the Bentham point, or the product, the Nash point), do not represent the best result for the theory of justice as fairness nor for the difference principle. In fact, when a curve OP begins to fall after having reached the highest point (i.e. after touching the line of higher justice), it means that an increase of utility of those who are better off no longer leads also to an improvement of those who are worse. Beyond this point (the threshold), if the individuals who are better off enrich themselves more, it would be necessary to redistribute their income to those who are worse off (*ceteris paribus* for what regards the other primary goods, and therefore assuming that the fact of the redistribution doesn't harm the fundamental liberties). In order to identify the threshold, it is necessary to understand exactly what primary goods are in practice.

3.4 Indeterminacy and the Four-Stage Sequence

Rawls offers a list of primary goods rather generic, and in *Justice as fairness* [2001, §51], confirms the flexibility of the category. The application of the difference principle to concrete cases would lead to unpredictable consequences if the index of primary goods were considered as a whole, rather than one dimension at a time (i.e. income, liberties and so on). H.L.A. Hart [1975] criticizes the indeterminacy in Rawls's conception of liberty and, as stated by Valeria Ottonelli in *Leggere Rawls*, he "pointed out that the principle remains completely undetermined: it is not clear which liberty should be guaranteed, and to what extent, until the citizens of a well-ordered society (and the parties in the «original position») will specify a list of purposes and activities that should enjoy special protection" (translation mine) [2010, 95]. The reference is to Rawls' first principle of justice, but, as said, if the liberties of the first principle are not accurately determined, this applies exactly in the same way to the difference principle, given that liberty is part of primary goods. Such criticism highlights even more how much Rawls's concept of primary goods appears obscure and, consequently, problematic in practice.

Actually, the indeterminacy of the index is not a problem in Rawls's theory, but a fundamental feature of it, without which the theory of justice as fairness would be even contradictory. In fact Rawls replies to Hart's criticism specifying a list of fundamental liberties [1993, VIII §1, 292] that can be achieved in two ways: historically and analytically. Nevertheless, the key point is not the list itself, since "the discriminating power of philosophical reflection at the level of the original position may soon run out. When this happens we should settle on the last preferred list and then specify that list further at the constitutional, legislative, and judicial stages, when general knowledge of social institutions and of society's circumstances is made known" (Rawls [1993, VIII, §1, 293]). Thus liberties would be specified in different stages and so, by analogy, even the rest of primary goods (and in general the index as a whole) could be specified in this way. This idea of various stages recalls the "four-stage sequence" (Rawls [1971, §31]), namely the framework Rawls adopts in order to "simplify the application of the two principles of justice" [1971, §31, 195]. Therefore it's plausible that the index of primary goods (not only liberties) should be determined through the four stages.

> *"Each stage is to represent an appropriate point of view from which certain kinds of questions are considered. Thus I suppose that after the parties have adopted the principles of justice in the original position, they move to a constitutional convention [...] It is at this stage that they weigh the justice of procedures for coping with diverse political views. Since the appropriate conception of justice has been agreed upon, the veil of ignorance in partially lifted"*
> John Rawls [1971, §31, 196-197]

The four stages are: the original position, the constitutional convention, the legislative stage, the last is "the application of rules to particular cases by judges and administrators, and the following of rules by citizens generally" [§31, 199]. It is important to note that at this last stage "everyone has complete access to all the facts. No limits on knowledge remain since the full system of rules has now been adopted and applies to persons in virtue of their characteristics and circumstances" [§31, 199][65]. Therefore primary goods, basically, would be determined in light of all general economic and social facts of a particular society, in a given situation. The veil of ignorance is already partially lifted in the constitutional convention stage, and even more, when the difference principle is applied in the other stages, contingent situations should be carefully considered, including the presence of various conceptions of good in the society and their own features.

---

[65] Rawls associates the first principle of justice to the stage of the constitutional convention, the second to the legislative one:
> *"The first principle of equal liberty is the primary standard for the constitutional convention. [...] Thus the constitution establishes a secure common status of equal citizenship and realizes political justice. The second principle comes into play at the stage of the legislature. [...] At this point the full range of general economic and social facts is brought to bear [...] Thus the priority of the first principle of justice to the second is reflected in the priority of the constitutional convention to the legislative stage"*
> John Rawls [1971, §31, 199]

The argument supporting the four-stage sequence is that "men's judgments and beliefs are likely to differ especially when their [of the citizens] interests are engaged. Therefore secondly, a citizen must decide which constitutional arrangements are just for reconciling conflicting opinions of justice" (Rawls [1971, §31, 195-196]). Rawls's theory offers a method to mediate among these interests (namely among different conceptions of the good) without proposing an alternative to these conceptions, as it might be a very specific list of primary goods. The purpose of the theory is in fact more general: ensuring neutral conditions so that the index of goods may actually be the result of a social agreement, in which contracting parties endorse their opinions and controversial conceptions of the goods. In fact, pure procedural justice (such as the original position[66]) does not intend to express a certain conception of good, but the political process shall be considered "as a machine which makes social decisions when the views of representatives and their constituents are fed into it"; the purpose of this machine is to "rank procedures for selecting which political opinion is to be enacted into law" [1971, §31, 196]. And these opinions, as observed, are determined by the conceptions of the good: judgments, beliefs and interests. For this reason, primary goods are ultimately determined by the social contract. This method perfectly suites the idea of neutrality as exposed in Charles Larmore's political liberalism. Therefore, in order to apply the index of primary goods in a factual context, we must move to further steps beyond the original position, up to the point where we have to vote (decide by voting) on the matter in question in a

---

[66] The original position is a "case of pure procedural justice", as Rawls explicates in *Political liberalism* [1993, II, §5.2, 73]. The subject is widely treated in *Theory* §14, where it is specified that the theory of justice as fairness intends to "apply the notion of pure procedural justice to distributive shares" [1971, §14, 86].

particular case[67]. At the legislative stage the "proposed bills are judged from the position of a representative legislator who, as always, does not know the particulars about himself" (Rawls [1971, §31, 198]), therefore a partial veil of ignorance remains. However, the representative legislator must choose, or mediate, among "proposed bills", which comes from citizens (or their representatives) with different conceptions of good. In some cases, we may even consider that what is called here "representative legislator" could be simply a machine that counts votes, and the measure that has the majority passes, provided that the statutes meet "not only the principles of justice but whatever limits are laid down in the constitution" [§31, 198].

Rawls therefore intentionally leaves the concept of index of primary goods as undetermined, but it could not be otherwise, if the theory of justice as fairness shall remain coherent with its neutral intent. As Rawls says: "on many questions of social and economic policy we must fall back upon a notion of quasi-pure procedural justice [...] This indeterminacy in the theory of justice is not in itself a defect. It is what we should expect" [1971, §31, 201]. There is disagreement among liberal and reasonable thinkers even on constitutional principles, while the difference principle, which should not appear even in a constitution (it cannot have legal value, and it must be a sort of preamble to the constitution instead[68]), can be compared to a

---

[67] Rawls in *Justice as Fairness* proposes the case of a parliamentary measure that allots public funds to preserve the beauty of nature in certain places. According to the principles of political liberalism, it is possible that arguments in favour of such a measure can be sustained on the basis of specific conceptions of good, as they could be perfectionism or utilitarianism: "some arguments in favour may rest on political values [...] political liberalism with its idea of public reason does not rule out as a reason the beauty of nature as such or the good of wildlife achieved by protecting its habitat. With the constitutional essentials all firmly in place, these matters may appropriately be put to a vote" [2001, §46.2, 152, n26].

[68] It is explained by Rawls in *Justice as Fairness*.

kind of aspiration – so to speak – which would inspire the legislature. The only stages in which there is no reasonable disagreement are: the original position (where each conception of the good is excluded from the veil of ignorance), the overlapping consensus (by definition), the general formulation of the principles of justice and, consequently, the idea of using the primary goods, rather than utility or other parameters, as an indicator of what are the needs of free and equal citizens. However, the index of the primary goods in a specific formulation – suitable for application in factual context – would be determined only by the social contract at different stages, provided that instances of the previous stages (the first is the original position) are observed. Rawls does not say it clearly, but this process would also lead to the fact that the social contract, in each stage, would determine the way in which the fundamental liberties, and consequently a specific characterisation of them, shall be guaranteed. The index (and so even the fundamental liberties) does not correspond to a conception of good supported by Rawls, nor by anyone. Determining what are the liberties that "provide the political and social condition essential for the adequate development and full exercise of the two moral powers of free and equal persons" [2001, §13.4, 45] is an issue that does not appear immediate nor thinkable without consulting the most important conceptions of good in the society. Even if to enunciate these liberties seems easy, the way in which they shall be regulated (under the

---

"A second worry is whether the fulfilment of the difference principle should be affirmed in a society's constitution. It seems that it should not, for this risks making it a constitutional essential which the courts are to interpret and enforce, and this task is not one they can perform well. Whether that principle is met requires a full understanding of how the economy works and is extremely difficult to settle with any exactness, although it may often be clear that it is not satisfied. Still, if there is sufficient agreement on the principle, it might be accepted as one of society's political aspirations in a preamble that lacks legal force (as with the U.S. Constitution)"
John Rawls [2001, §49,5, 162]

constitutional, legislative and jurisprudential stages) has serious implications on the actual notions underlying those enunciations.

3.5   The right of Property in Rawls' Theory

Let's make an example regarding the right of property: it is a primary good since it is included among the social basis of self-respect (Rawls [2001, §32.6, 114]). This right is historically highly discussed, from the libertarian theory of the "entitlement" of Nozick [1974][69] to Marxist or socialist theories[70]. The theory of justice as fairness promotes the property as the right "to hold and to have the exclusive use of personal property" (Rawls [2001, §32.6, 114]. But how shall be determined this concept in light of the practical and normative regulation of the right within the society? Would it be closer to the libertarian or the socialist version, or again, entirely different from both? According to Rawls, this concept does not exclude nor support the wider conceptions of "private property" or "social property" of means of production and natural resources: "these wider conception of property are not used because they are not necessary for the adequate development and full exercise of moral powers, and so are not an essential social basis of self-respect. They may, however, still be justified. This depends on existing historical and social conditions" [2001, §32.6, 114]. This underlies the fact that conceptions of the good present in society, varying from one society to another, can lead to a very different choice of

---

[69] It is clear that if the State applies any redistribution (except the eventual legitimation given by the principle of "rectification of injustice") is violating the principles of justice of Nozick's entitlement theory.

[70] Rawls speaks about "equal right to participate in the control of the means of production and of natural resources" [2001, §32.6,114].

primary goods (including the right to property), depending on the outcome of the deliberations at each stage: "further specification of the rights to property is to be made at the legislative stage, assuming the basic rights and liberties are maintained" [§32.6, 114]. Probably, if it happened to apply the theory of justice as fairness to a society where the right of private property is completely extraneous to the moral and political conceptions of its members (it doesn't matter if this type of society really exists or has ever existed: we can think of something like a particular primitive society in the Amazon) then among the primary goods there wouldn't be this right indeed. This conclusion could be reached just by virtue of pure procedural justice. On the other hand, applying the principles of justice as fairness to a society alike the American Far West (under the assumption that it corresponds to what some libertarian intellectuals have described[71]), among the primary goods would appear indeed some property right similar to what Nozick proposed in the entitlement theory. This happens only in case, perhaps unrealistic, that in the Far West there was total conformity between the current social condition and the conceptions of good belonging to those who lived there. This conformity could depend on the fact that, in those societies, there were mostly individuals characterized by a careerist or

---

[71] Lottieri refers to several authors: Guglielmo Piombini, *Far West: l'epoca libertaria della storia americana*, Federalismo & Società, year IV, n. 3, 1997; Anderson T. L. and Hill P. J., *An American Experiment in Anarcho-Capitalism: «The Not so Wild, Wild West»*, The Journal of Libertarian Studies, year III, n. 1, 1979.

"a world essentially libertarian, for example, was the American Wild West, where the law enforcement and security were insured by private parties: and all this happened (in spite of what one believes and despite the filmography of Hollywood) in an effective, civil and inexpensive way, considering that – in relation to the resident population – the number of crimes committed in the territories not yet nationalized was much lower than the ones in the East Coast, placed under the control of Washington" (translation mine)
Carlo Lottieri [2001, 243]

Darwinist spirit[72] or, easier, individuals who had already developed an attachment to the "basic structure" of that libertarian society (which in such case would have reached the stability[73]), which presents, among few but effective rules, a kind of right of private property comparable to Nozick's entitlement theory, no matter how this right is born or developed. It may be that, in a libertarian society of this kind, the concept of liberty itself (determined by the conceptions of good of those who live there) implies, thanks to the priority of the first principle on the second, also immunity from any coercive redistribution of property by the State: liberty would be understood as liberty from aggression of the State, since regulation is seen as a threat and taxation as a real theft[74]. In this type of hypothetical society the idea of neutrality towards different conceptions of good can lead to the decision to grant the right of property as described, since everyone agrees on it and there is no conflict among the various conceptions of good. These considerations means nothing by themselves (because it would never arise, for example, the opportunity to apply Rawls' theory to an Amazon primitive society, nor to a people composed of only libertarians), rather they are functional to understand that "the question of private property in the means of production or their social

---

[72]This assumption is just an example. It's not relevant for the aim of this essay to verify the truth of this fact. It is not certain at all that such people would adopt a "basic structure" of society of this kind. Anyway, for the notion of social Darwinism (or Spencerism), the reference is to the sociological theory of Herbert Spencer.

[73] An aim of the theory of justice as fairness is to achieve public support and therefore the stability:

"*It is an important feature of a conception of justice that it should generate its own support. That is, its principles should be such that when they are embodied in the basic structure of society, men tend to acquire the corresponding sense of justice. Given the principles of moral learning, men develop a desire to act in accordance with its principles. In this case a conception of justice is stable*" John Rawls [1971, §24, 138]

[74]According to Rothbard [1973] taxation is theft, conscription is slavery, and war is mass murder.

ownership and similar questions are not settled at the level of the first principles of justice, but depend upon the traditions and social institutions of a country and its particular problems and historical circumstances" (Rawls [1993, VIII, §9, 338]). The conclusion achieved on the right of property can be easily extended, by analogy, to the other primary goods and to the index as a whole. The characteristic of indeterminacy of the index (and therefore of the application of the difference principle), is not only suitable for the theory of justice as fairness, but necessary. It's even essential to the conservation of neutrality towards different conceptions of good for the society. As Larmore says, "Rawls's original position is best understood as a position of neutrality, so one might think here of his argument for the difference principle" [1987, 44]. In light of the above, it's possible to understand why Buchanan [1984] and Lomasky [2005] think that starting from the principle of the greatest equal liberty proposed by Rawls we are forced to come to a quasi-libertarian solution[75]. The problem is that often libertarians claim that their own conception of the good is to determine the social choice of an index of primary goods, or the right scheme of cooperation. They do not take into account that in societies where there is not unanimous consent on such conception of good (as the society in which we live, for which is designed the Rawlsian theory) it is also necessary to justify the proposed principles to everyone. The jusnaturalism by which libertarians support their ideals is not enough, since it may appear nothing

---

[75] See Lottieri [2001, 168]. Indeed a quasi-libertarian solution is not the outcome Rawls expects for the present American society based on the theory of justice as fairness. It is clear that he admits redistribution (through coercion of the State). In fact, even if the difference principle should not appear in a constitution, there it would be at least a guaranteed social minimum, as Rawls writes in *Justice as fairness*: "What should be a constitutional essential is an assurance of a social minimum covering at least the basic human needs, as specified in §38.3-4. For it is reasonably obvious that the difference principle is rather blatantly violated when that minimum is not guaranteed" [§49,5, 162].

more than a kind of new theology. It also applies to other forms of political espressivism such as Sandel's communitarianism. On the contrary, according to political liberalism, the principles proposed by libertarians and communitarians may be applied only if supported from a neutral position: entailing rational dialogue and equal respect, and instituting "only the least abridgment of neutrality necessary for making decision possible". On the contrary, the only way to affirm these principles without presenting a neutral justification is imposing them by force (of any kind, such as the oppression by the State).

3.6   Inequalities and Social Stability

The practical application of the difference principle involves the complicated effort of weighing all the rights, as a whole – through the four stage sequence – of each representative individual, and redresses the largest violations, or major situations of injustice, in a long-term perspective. In a nutshell, its concern is to prevent or repair the greatest injustice, exactly because the "least-advantaged" are those who suffer the greatest injustice: according to the analysis presented in this essay, it is precisely in this way that we can understand the difference principle. But what the greatest injustice consists in inevitably depends on the current culture and beliefs within society. For this reason, the difference principle, in the end, plays nothing but a role of guarantee for the rights (without explicit definition of what they are in practice) of each representative individual. In virtue of its function it represents, ultimately, a liberal warranty of the rights of citizens.

Indeterminacy of primary goods imply an interpretation of the principle in a procedural way, considering what is right or wrong on the basis of a particular "measure", given by a procedure commonly considered valid, for instance the method of majority rule. The difference principle could either work redressing the greatest injustices, or just protecting people from the greatest injustices (without redressing anything). In the first case, it implies redistribution; in the second it guarantees those rights connected to what Berlin (inspired by Benjamin Constant) defined "negative liberty" (Berlin [1958]). It is possible to imagine exceptional context in which negative liberties would be considered the only rights entitled to be protected, for instance due to the very particular culture of a libertarian society. This means that the difference principle is such undetermined that we could even figure out imaginary cases in which redistribution isn't legitimate at all. In fact it ultimately represents a procedural norm stating: "we shall prevent the greatest injustice", which embodies different substantive meanings, from case to case, depending on what is the conception of justice of a particular society. In this context, Harsanyi's criticism [1975] falters. He complains, misrepresenting the Rawlsian principle, that Rawls assumes the parties in the original position would be maximally risk-averse: only thanks to this reason they would choose a principle that maximizes the condition of the poorest. But income distribution is a completely different issue with respect to the difference principle. Just to provide an extreme-case example, if libertarians think that what's most unjust is losing liberties, in their perspective even a billionaire entrepreneur may be "the worse off" with respect to a destitute, if the State limits in some way her possibilities of investment. Then, in the ideal model of a stereotyped libertarian society (assuming it may exist), the fact of maximizing the condition of the weakest – when "weakest" refers to an extreme lack of liberties – consists in maximizing the liberties *de facto* for the entire society. It's not a really different issue from the fact of "weighing individual preferences" or defining legitimate or illegitimate interests, before including them in the "social calculation" (as all utilitarians including Harsanyi do in some way – according to

Villani). We all believe in some principles that are considered, by ourselves, of utmost importance: with regard to these, no rational person is disposed to risk, no matter how strong our aversion for the risk is.

The principle is rather undetermined, in the sense that it doesn't seem to propose a particular conception of primary goods. But is this characteristic of indeterminacy enough to consider the principle neutral towards controversial conceptions of the good life? Indeed, indeterminacy of the principle doesn't imply it embodies only a procedural conception of justice, excluding other moral arguments. On the contrary, it expresses a specific conception of good, maybe conflicting with other ideals: it claims not only respect for others, but also a "concern for the weakest", though independent of how is defined the "weakness". According to Larmore and Rawls, basic assumptions of the justification of political liberalism are rationality and reasonableness (the last well represented by the ideal of equal respect): are these prerequisites sufficient in order to justify this kind of concern?

Although a concern for the weakest might not be in moral terms as fundamental as equal respect, it presents anyway a high level of neutrality[76]. For instance, the difference principle might be neutrally defended even from possible criticisms by social Darwinism or Spencerism. Those theories are supposed to endorse the law of the strongest against a moral interest for the weakest, who are left to succumb. But the mere law of the strongest – without any limit (into anarchic framework) – cannot fit for equal respect. Then a Darwinist perspective opens two possible scenarios: 1) it doesn't comply with equal respect, and in this case it's not reasonable; or 2) it simply expresses a concern (which prevails on other kind of interests but doesn't exceed the equal respect) for merits and opportunity to

---

[76] As seen in the second chapter, Larmore speaks about the principle of "higher neutrality" (see Larmore [1987, 68]).

implement talents[77]. The last category is the only one we need to discuss, and necessarily presumes a framework of rules with the aim of ensuring a fair, or legitimate, competition. Even Nozick's entitlement theory cannot be implemented without rules and monitors. But a framework of rules ultimately defines a conception of justice, and the one who suffers the greatest injustice (it occurs when the most important rules are broken) can be considered "the weakest". Therefore, the difference principle, in its most abstract intension, can be neutrally justified even in the perspective of a Darwinist conception of good life, provided that a Darwinist conception doesn't reject equal respect.

However neutral, there are people who might not agree on the moral implication of the difference principle. For those, another kind of justification may be proposed. Difference in our society is seen as unfair unless it is justified in some way: that's a matter of fact in our society, since it holds for the many. If citizens wouldn't feel morally committed in preventing or repairing the greatest injustices of the least-advantaged – explaining the moral justifications of differences, or the moral reasons by which they have to be redressed – they probably wouldn't even start a debate on these problems. A system which doesn't prompt the discussion about something that is commonly considered unfair, is unlikely to be a stable system. Without justifying differences between worse off and better off, the system is more prone to collapse. It has nothing to do with ought-statements, since without such system, simply, a liberal society would always run into the threat of collapsing. Therefore the difference principle, as method to justify inequalities among various conditions of citizens, is crucial for the stability of society. Where difference is unfair, the principle demands to be redressed, but before playing

---

[77] The assumption behind (not necessarily true) is that a social theory might coherently be called Darwinist and at the same time complying with the principle of equal respect.

this function, it develops a prudential task, aimed to maintain the stability, just because it offers citizens the perception that difference has a reason to be. Even libertarians should recognize that this is a good expedient (maybe because of its psychological mechanism) to legitimate differences to the worse off. But what libertarians seem to ignore is that, without a justification of differences, their liberties would be always jeopardized. A liberal society cannot really stand if most of citizens do not perceive wide differences among their conditions as fair.

In conclusion, the difference principle establishes a reciprocity bond between – say – rich and poor (considering income dimension) or, at least, it "interprets" this connection, or interdependence (if it is supposed to exist) between rich and poor, as a solidarity bond. But the mere fact of interpretation can have significant influence if the principle is endorsed by institutions, for in a well-ordered society "social institutions generate an effective supporting sense of justice" (Rawls [1999, 234]) and norms with institutional recognition are naturally strengthened in the "cultural background" of society. Then the difference principle may even represent a sort of *original Compact*, with a function of "social glue", between rich and poor, stronger and weaker, binding one to another. As Larmore says, reasonableness (equal respect) is not sufficient in order to justify political liberalism, but even an *original Compact* is necessary, without which we cannot see the motivation to start a rational conversation. If the rich doesn't perceive to be socially interconnected with the poor, they probably wouldn't start a debate on inequalities issues, leaving room for other ways of resolving the differences, so endangering the stability of the system.

One last point has to be analysed, which Dworkin in *A Matter of Principle* [1985] helps us to point out. As already highlighted, if a laissez-faire system is supposed to better perform than a welfarist system, improving the condition of the worst off in the long run, then the difference principle would simply represent a justification of differences, without redressing them. According to Dworkin those propositions represent a "doubtful" empirical claim, though it is a popular argument among libertarians[78]. If this claim was true, then libertarians would legitimately assert that the difference principle is better implemented in a laissez-faire system[79]. The justification of differences would be typically utilitarian: it "asks some people to accept lives of great poverty and despair, with no prospect of a useful future, just in order that the great bulk of the community may have a more ample measure of what they are forever denied" (Dworkin [1985, 210]). The problem is that if people do not see an immediate benefit for themselves or their descendants, they wouldn't easily accept this mechanism. Dworkin says that "the present poor are asked to sacrifice in favour of their fellow citizens now, in order to prevent a much greater injustice, to many more citizens, later" [1985, 100]. He raises an objection to this argument:

> *"Treating people as equals requires a more active conception of membership. If people are asked to sacrifice for their community, they must be offered some reason why the community which benefits from that sacrifice is their community; there must be some reason why, for example, the unemployed blacks of Detroit should take more interest in either the public virtue or the future generations of Michigan than they do in those of Mali [...One] can identify himself with the future of the community and accept present deprivation as sacrifice rather than tyranny, only if he has some power to help determine the shape of that future, and only if the promised prosperity will provide at least equal benefit to the*

---

[78] The "empirical claim" will be further considered in §4.4, commenting Jason Brennan's thought experiment represented in *Figure 4*.

[79] It would also apply in case primary goods consisted just in wealth or income. If the empirical claim is true, libertarians wouldn't need to raise the argument that property rights are included among primary goods in order to refute redistribution policies in the application of the difference principle.

*smaller, more immediate communities for which he feels special
responsibilities, for example, his family, his descendants, and, if the
society is one that has made this important to him, his race"*
Ronald Dworkin [1985, 211]

If this concern is enough in order to legitimate a redistributive
intervention by public authorities, it depends either on
considerations about political stability of the system and
economic analysis of the correctness of the libertarian "empirical
claim". However, the pursuit of political stability shouldn't be
pretext for heavier State intervention in the name of other issues
of social justice.

3.7   Democratic Process

As it has been exposed, the democratic procedures are
fundamental in the practical application of the principle, since it
is supposed to be applied in our society, that is nothing but a
democratic society. Considered the indeterminacy of the primary
goods, it seems that the outcome of a democratic process might
have a central role in determining the conception of "weakness"
and therefore what is actually regulated by the difference
principle. Democracy is Rawls' premise, taken as a matter of
fact, he doesn't deal with the goodness of this ideal of political
participation. Nonetheless, even democracy should be justified
in a neutral way.

Each kind of political organizations, regimes or societies shall
preserve itself and achieve stability in order to pursue, in
practice, its ideals. This must be reckoned in order to
approximate reality to our ideals, even if the reaching for stability
sometimes forces to leave aside part of our wishes. A non-
merely utopian model, but effectively feasible one, must take
into account the fact of stability, related to empirical conditions.
For this reason a practical and substantive interpretation of the

difference principle cannot be detached from the outcome of a democratic process (not meant as a method of majority rule, but as the actual entire procedure of democracy, even constituted by checks and balances); otherwise it would lead to unstable outcomes. One of the goals of every model of political organization (included liberalism) is stability: we could hardly think of a regime, whether real or ideal, that wouldn't aim to the minimization of the number of opponents, adverse ideals, or any factors threatening its survival. These factors, in our society, may be inequality, lack of liberties, lack of security, economic inefficiencies, corruption, moral decay, and so on. Minimizing these conditions regimes are more stable and even fairer. Justice – or at least what is perceived just – and stability are strictly correlated: no social system can be just if unstable. According to the ideal stereotypes, a libertarian system is considered "fair" by its supporters because it guarantees liberties related to self-ownership; a socialist system because it grants survival to everybody under acceptable conditions; a communist system because it grants equality, and so on. All these ideals are highly contested and no one can easily overcome the respective alternatives. On the contrary, in our modern western countries most of people – with few exceptions – think of democracy as the right political system. Democracy might be considered a "fair" method of decision process because it offers everybody the possibility to participate to political process of deliberation, public choice, government, et cetera. But the success of democracy doesn't depend on its moral qualities, rather it depends on its relative stability, and maybe this fact is ignored by the many. In fact, from an ideal point of view, it's difficult to demonstrate that democracy is fairer than aristocracy, for instance. It would be logic that administrators should be the ones who are better in administrating, and from a merely theoretical or ideal point of view, under aristocracy the government is in the hands of the άριστοι (*aristoi*), namely the most excellent, the best administrators: the ones who are able to better realize the principles of justice. We can object that these principles of justice are not given ex-ante, therefore democracy may represent a procedure to identify them. But once identified these principles, why should they be achieved by elected authorities? The "goodness" of the ideal of political participation is not so evident. The literature developed stemming from Arrow's theory[80] is exemplificative of these arguments. As Przeworsky states, "democracy is not rational, in the eighteenth-century sense of the term" (1999, 25), "it thus seems that choosing rulers by elections does not assure either rationality, or representation, or equality" (1999, 43). In other words, as summarized by Tsebelis:

> *"there is nothing that can be defined as the common good to be maximized (existence). If there were, the democratic process does not necessarily identify it (convergence), and if it did, democracy is not the only system that does (uniqueness) [...] Przeworski goes on to demonstrate that even this substandard system* [a minimal conception of democracy] *under certain conditions presents one significant advantage: that the losers in an election may prefer to wait until the next round rather than to revolt against the system. This peaceful preservation property a fortiori holds for Schumpeterian democracy,*[81] *where citizens control electoral sanctions and representatives know that reelection depend on responsiveness"*
>
> George Tsebelis [2002, 67]

---

[80] According to Arrow (1951) there is, in social life, a trade-off between social rationality and the concentration of power. Any mechanism which translates the preferences of *rational* individuals into a *coherent* group preference (namely, respecting some minimal conditions – no further analysed here) is either dictatorial (independent of distinguished individual) or incoherent. But the method of "majority rule" holds precisely on the minimal conditions mentioned by Arrow (cf May [1952]), so it is incoherent: it violates rationality assumption, at least on some occasions.

[81] According to Schumpeter's "economical model of democracy" (1950), democracy is simply a matter of leaders competing for votes.

Democracy seems stable, at least in western countries after the Second World War, and it is probably due to the fact that it has already generated an effective supporting sense of justice in citizens' cultural background. This also implies a good reason for which political liberalism shall support democracy: without stability, neutrality couldn't be, because the rules and the government conduct couldn't be predictable, and predictability itself confers a certain grade of neutrality[82]. There are cases in which liberalism and democracy present conflicting ideals, for instance the tyranny of the majority, but given some defined limits of the State they can freely go hand in hand. Furthermore, the ideal of participation could be neutrally justified under a liberal perspective, and it's probably the best way to justify democracy: democratic participation can be defended as the best means for insuring that the State does remain neutral toward the intrinsic worth of all ideals of good life (Larmore [1987, 130]; Schumpeter [1950, 232-302]). By historical and analytical examinations, it seems that does not exist other regime achieving these liberal goals better than democracy. Finally, democracy itself represents an *original Compact*, since it leads citizen to dialogue (competing for votes means convincing the electors), while equal respect explains why to undertake it in a rational way. In this respect, the role of the difference principle within political liberalism is comparable to the role of democracy; they are even tied together, since democratic procedures affect the substantive meaning of the principle. They both represent an *original Compact* which doesn't rest on the same basis of neutrality, that are rationality and reasonableness. Instead they are instruments to achieve stability: since it's not possible to actually grant neutrality without stability, they represent, in a way, a very important element of neutrality, that is what allows its existence in an empirical context.

---

[82] See the first chapter §1.7, or Larmore [1987, 40]

4   The Moral Foundation of Liberty

We defined equal respect as the fundamental principle of justice. Liberalism – despite what the name suggests – ultimately relies on the ideal of equality rather than liberty, which has only a derivative role. We should be free to pursue our own conception of the good life because we are worthy of equal respect (§2.2). In fact equal respect requires us to rationally discuss about the political rules and to establish neutral institutions with respect to controversial conceptions of the good life (§2.1): given neutral institutions, citizens are free to choose to lead the life they desire. In this way, liberty is understood as freedom from interference (by public institutions or other people's actions) in citizen's choices. Citizens cannot afford whatever kind of life they may desire and institutions shouldn't provide them the possibilities to live whatever kind of life, guaranteeing in this way equal success, or welfare, to citizens (§2.6). In a liberal system, since institutions do not advantage nor promote any particular conception, people pay the price of the life they have decided to lead, measured in what others give up in order that they can do so (§2.7). If political institutions redistributed resources (or fixed the price of some good), in order to promote a person's choice of life, it would even influence or hinder other persons' choice of life, provoking in this way distortions in the entire system of pricing. Since prices represent the values people attribute to other's actions and services, a political intervention would interfere with the conceptions of the good life in which those values are assessed.

4.1   Equal opportunity and Inheritance Tax

If people choices were constrained only by what their deliberate decisions cost others, these constraints would limit everybody in the same, equal, way. Then people would be equally free to choose the life they desire, and the neutral requirement of equal respect would be observed. Nonetheless, other conditions may affect people' choices producing other – unequal – kind of constraints: they may be disease, bad luck, talents, or different initial endowments of resources. The purpose of mitigating the differences in endowments can be also seen as the pursuit of equal opportunity of citizens to live their life as they choose, being constrained only by what their decisions cost others, instead of being initially (dis)advantaged by their endowments. In the free market framework required by a liberal State, to secure citizens from accidents, disease or bad luck, each one should be aware of the possibility to take out an insurance and, at least in some cases, which Dworkin calls "brutal luck", the insurance scheme is to be funded by general taxation (§2.7). The case of optional luck instead is ascribable to a problem of different life choices, since everyone can choose to take out an insurance or to tempt fate. Anyway, brutal luck is not the only justification of tax imposition, since a liberal State requires a publicly funded education system. Even if citizens shall be free to choose how to educate their children[83], they should at least "understand the political conception" (even if they shouldn't be necessarily educated to a comprehensive liberal conception, see §2.2). Then children's education shall include such things as knowledge of their constitutional and civic rights. For example

---

[83] School vouchers may be a proper means to conciliate freedom of education and the requirement of a liberal State to educate citizens to understand the political conception. The vouchers would be spendable only in those school providing students the basic knowledge of their constitutional and civic rights, explaining that liberty of conscience exists in their society and that apostasy is not a legal crime.

citizens shall know that apostasy is not a legal crime, so that it doesn't represent an additional constraint when they undertake important life choices. We should never forget that taxes, as a redistributive measure, inevitably influence in some way people's choices, then they should be the less distortive possible: income tax is preferred to indirect, property and labor tax[84].

If citizens started their lives each endowed with the same talents and the same amount of resources, a laissez-faire economic system would be perfectly compatible with Dworkin's conception of equality of resources, with the only exception of the compulsory tax covering the insurance system and the costs of public education. Resource endowment is also affected by talents, which do not depend (not entirely) on deliberate decisions and citizens' ambitions. This represents another source of unequal constraints to citizens' life choices. To mitigate differences in endowments generated by talents is a highly sensitive issue Dworkin's conception of insurance cannot properly deal with, as explained in §2.7. Instead Rawls' difference principle could establish the general framework in which these issues have to be considered, since it doesn't disregard considerations of economic efficiency (an inefficient system would lower the expected welfare of future or present worst off generations, see §3.2 and §4.4). The specific policies adopted to promote equal opportunities against different endowments of talents may include the promotion of active training programs (education is the best way to increase opportunities) and unemployment insurance[85], but here the

---

[84] Under the assumption that indirect taxation has more tendency to produce substitution effects on consumption than direct income taxation

[85] Welfare policies may institute labour market training programme for unemployed people in which they are committed to individual action plans and activities in seeking a suitable job (which may include apprenticeship and free work). Indeed, at the same time a minimum income scheme has to be established, with strict eligibility criteria to

philosophical speculation leaves the field to comparative politics and economic analysis, and this topics are not treated further. Talents are not the most important source of inequalities. Even if people started with the same amount of resources, life choices would inevitably produce inequalities in the endowment within the course of a person's life. This inequalities are justified by the conception of equality outlined, but may be handed down to future generations in this way increasing over time, hindering equal opportunity and producing inequalities in the amount of resources new generations are initially endowed with. The problem is that we cannot determine a "starting point" in people's life where they could be endowed with the same amount of resources, since if political institutions equalized the endowment of all citizens at a certain point in time, citizens' past life choices would be completely upset by this political intervention[86]. There are other ways to approximate reality to the

---

avoid moral hazard of the recipients: first, it should be always much more profitable for everybody to have an income from work compared to have an income from transfers, which may also decrease over time, such that pressure is put on the recipients to seek to find and accept job offers; second, persons shall be entitled to unemployment benefits only if they demonstrate readiness to accept an offered job and if they participate to the labour market training programs. These are only suggestions inspired by the Swedish welfare system. See for example:

- Halleröd B. (2009), *Minimum income Schemes: Sweden*, European Commission;
- Bjorklund A., Freeman R. B. (1994), *Generating Equality and Eliminating Poverty, The Swedish Way*, NBER Working Paper n. 4945.

[86] For this reason Dworkin states that we must reject the "starting-gate theory":

"we must reject the starting-gate theory and recognize that the requirements of equality (in the real world at least) pull in opposite direction. On the one hand we must, on pain of violating equality, allow the distribution of resources at any particular moment to be (as we might say) ambition-sensitive. It must, that is, reflect the cost or benefit to others of the choices people make so that, for example, those who choose to invest rather than consume, or to consume less expensively rather than more, or to work in more rather than less profitable ways must be permitted to retain the gains that flow from these decisions in an

ideal of equality or resources. Institutions have to impose inheritance taxes with the redistributive purpose of guaranteeing equality of opportunity, at the same time preserving – as much as possible – the life choices of individuals and their conceptions of the good life. A good idea to meet this goal is suggested by Nozick in *The Examined Life* (1989), where he endorses a completely different view from the libertarianism (explained in §4.2) proposed in *Anarchy, State and Utopia* (1974).

According to Nozick [1989, 28], there is no bond stronger than being a parent. Children themselves are a part of one's substance, raising them gives one's life substance: "Parents reside within their children's unconscious, children in their parents' bodies [...] If adolescence is sometimes marked by rebelling against one's parents and adulthood by becoming independent of them, what marks maturity is becoming a parent to them" [29]. Bequeathing something to others is an expression of caring about them, and it intensifies those bonds. It also marks, and perhaps sometimes creates, an "extended identity" [31]. The receivers – children, grandchildren, friends or whoever – need not have earned what they receive. Although to some extent they may have earned the continuing affection of the bequeather, it is the donor who has earned the right to mark and serve her relational bonds by bequeathal. The conception of the good life of one person may include special concerns for the beloved ones: she could have worked hard over the course of her life only with the purpose of securing them a comfortable life. One may have the desire to leave something behind after death, a sign of her reputation and feats, a family which keeps vivid her memory, also through the wealth bequeathed. Nozick states that Hegel and many other philosophers "have commented on the ways in which property earned or created is

---

equal auction followed by free trade"
Ronald Dworkin [2000, 89]

an expression of the self and a component of it, so that one's identity or personality can become embued or extended in such a creation" [31]. When the original creator or earner passes something on, a considerable portion of herself participates in and constitutes this act.

Yet Nozick recognizes that bequests that are received sometimes then are passed on for generations to persons unknown to the original earner and donor, producing continuing inequalities of wealth and position, and the resulting inequalities seem unfair. One possible solution would be to restructure an institution of inheritance so that taxes will subtract from the possessions people can bequeath the value of what they themselves have received through bequests. The monetary value of what one had received in inheritance would be calculated in contemporaneous currency, corrected for inflation or deflation but not including actual or imputed interest earned.

> *"People then could leave to others only the amount they themselves have added to (the amount of) their own inheritance. Someone could bequeath to anyone she chose – mate, children, grandchildren, friends, etc. (We might add the further limitation that these all be existing people – or gestating ones – to whom there already can be actual ties and relations.) However, those who receive will not similarly be allowed to pass that on, although they will be able to pass on to whomever they choose what they themselves have earned and added. An inheritance could not cascade down the generations"*
> Robert Nozick [1989, 30-31]

There are several problems with the subtraction rule, Nozick points out two of them [31]: first, it does not perfectly disentangle what the next generation has managed itself to contribute, because inheriting wealth may make it easier to amass more; second, how would the proposal avoid providing an incentive for squandering to those whose wealth near the end of their lives is not far above the amount taxes would subtract? A third issue is even more remarkable: only currencies (or quotas, assets, obligations, participations in businesses) are to be subtracted, or even goods and properties such as real estate? If real estate is liable to be subtracted, then the following kind of problem may rise. Suppose my grandfather built a restaurant (or a house) and all members in my family worked (lived) there for their entire life. When my father dies, I'm not entitled to the ownership of the restaurant (the house) where I spent my whole life and efforts and which evokes to me a sense of belonging to my family. That place could be of fundamental importance in pursuing the purposes I may retain as essential in my conception of the good life. I may also feel morally obliged to perform the role of restaurant man and to bring forth properly the activity, feeling a sort of "vocation" and responsibility towards my "ancestors". On the other hand, if real estate or other kind of goods were excluded by the subtraction rule, people would try to convert currencies in real estate, in this way bequeathing a larger portion of their properties, provoking disastrous distortions in the economy. For all these reasons the simple subtraction rule cannot be implemented. However, a similar solution can be found: an inheritance tax may be established taking into account, as far as possible, how much a person earned or created and how much inherited, applying on this base different tax rates. If this solution is achievable in practice and public authorities find an efficient way to prevent too many individuals from being able to circumvent this taxation, it would represent the best way to finance the goals the State has to accomplish, since it is far less distortive than other ways of taxation. Even if it doesn't seem compatible with Nozick's principle of justice in transfer (see §4.2), all libertarian minarchists[87] recognize some governmental institutions have to be financed: the military, police and courts. Since some kind of taxation has to be imposed, this inheritance

---

[87] According to minarchism the State ought to exist and its only legitimate function is the protection of individuals from aggression, theft, breach of contract, and fraud.

tax has the virtue of promoting individual's merits and efforts without disturbing individuals' deliberate decisions in pursuing their conceptions of the good life. In few words, it would represent the most neutral kind of taxation.

Nozick is not the only supporter of a laissez-faire economic system who also is in favor of inheritance tax. Buchanan favored a high inheritance tax, which he believed is needed to retain widespread support for the market system. As Geoffrey Brennan writes, Buchanan believed rather passionately in confiscatory estate and gift duties: "he reckoned that inherited wealth (though not self-made or first-generation wealth) violates basic equality of opportunity, and his enmity towards dynasties was notable" (Brennan [2013, 8]). Hayek could have been in favour of inheritance taxes too: "inheritance taxes could, of course, be made an instrument toward greater social mobility and greater dispersion of property and, consequently, may have to be regarded as important tools of a truly liberal policy which ought not to stand condemned by the abuse which has been made of it." (Hayek [2009, 118]). What is important is that the inheritance tax shall not be so high as to induce people to squander their wealth near the end of their lives, nor so high as to impede bonds between parents and children to be honored properly. Providing these conditions, inheritance taxes with different tax rates (on the basis of how much a person inherited and earned) may represent a system that may conciliate the demand of equal opportunity given by the conception of equality of resources (and the difference principle) and the demand of equal respect towards the conceptions of the good life. As it has exposed, a system of taxation of this kind can obtain broad approval from different parts in present society, also from the supporter of laissez-faire economics. Indeed, there are libertarian positions incompatible with any kind of taxation, as Rothbard's anarcho-capitalism proposed in *Ethics of Liberty* (1982): each man is entitled to "full and 100 percent selfownership" [1998, 45],

"Taxation is theft purely and simply even though it is theft on a grand and colossal scale which no acknowledged criminals could hope to match" [162] and the State is "the most extensive criminal (and hence the most immoral) group in society" [174]. Nozick in *Anarchy, State, and Utopia* (1974) advocated the presence of a minimal State as "night watchman", that guarantees property rights but cannot levy any inheritance tax, due to the principle of justice in transfer. Since a demonstration of the moral unjustifiability of Nozick's minarchism applies even to Rothbard's anarchism, next paragraphs focus only on Nozick's entitlement theory of justice, moving criticism against its moral foundation (§4.3).

4.2   The Libertarian Paradigm

The fundamental assumptions of a libertarian ethic are the concepts of "self-ownership" and "original acquisition". People own themselves and therefore their own labor. When a person works, that labor enters into the object. Thus, the object becomes the property of that person. It results in the "original" acquisition of a property or estate which has never been the property of another. According to Locke in the *Second treatise on Government* [1689, b], property originally comes about by the exertion of labor upon natural resources. It may occur when an entirely new proprietary right has been created: acquisition of a copyright owned by an author is an example of this kind of acquisition, for a new *res* has only just came into existence. In other cases original acquisition can occur when the *res* have been *res nullius*, owned by nobody: the discovery of an uninhabited land, or of an abandoned item.

Nozick in *Anarchy, State, and Utopia* built a theory of justice on the following assumptions, which he calls the "entitlement theory". There are three principles of justice:

"(1) A person who acquires a holding in accordance with the principle of justice in acquisition is entitled to that holding.
(2) A person who acquires a holding in accordance with the principle of justice in transfer, from someone else entitled to the holding, is entitled to the holding.
(3) No one is entitled to a holding except by (repeated) applications of (1) and (2)"
Robert Nozick [1974, 151]

Justice in transfer regards essentially the voluntary exchange from one person to another. In fact the owner can dispose of the good as she wants, including the sale and purchase, gift or destruction of the good. What matters is that those actions are always voluntarily subscribed by the owner. The existence of past injustice (previous violations of the first two principles of justice in holdings) requires the third principle of rectification of injustice in holdings: "Some people steal from others, or defraud them, or enslave them seizing their product and preventing them from living as they choose, or forcibly exclude others from competing in exchanges" [1974, 152]. Then who stole will be forced by institutions (whether they are private or public entities) to return the stolen goods. Citizens cannot be forced to pay taxes, even if the State intends to pursue noble purposes, such as economic efficiency, equity, or other conceptions of justice unrelated to the principles listed by Nozick. He states that the three principles of justice are "historical", for they regard the way property is chronologically acquired, exchanged, donated or destroyed: "whether a distribution is just depends upon how it came about" [1974, 153]. Unhistorical principles of justice are called "patterned", because they specify that a distribution is to vary along with some dimension and the justice of that distribution is "judged by some structural principle(s)" [153]. These principles are, let's say, "drawn on a model", because they are intended to make the distribution result into what determined by a certain "ideal" model (or pattern). Contemporary States are pursuing, or attempting to pursue, thousands of patterned principles concerning fairness, equality, merit, but also economic efficiency. An example of patterned principle is the distribution according to moral merit: "no person should have a greater share than anyone whose moral merit is greater" [156]. Nozick recalls Hayek's discussion of patterned principles, arguing that we cannot know enough about each person's situation to distribute to each according to her moral merit [158]: "our objection is against all attempts to impress upon society a deliberately chosen pattern of distribution, whether it be an order of equality or of inequality" (Hayek [1960, 87]). Nonetheless, Hayek proposes a pattern of distribution in accordance with "value" (the perceived value of a person's actions and services to others) rather than moral merit: "to each according to how much he benefits others who have the resources for benefiting those who benefit them", or alternatively: "from each as they choose, to each as they are chosen" (Nozick [1974, 160]). Even though it is a patterned principle, it is compatible with Nozick's historical principles of justice. In fact the parts involved in the transaction attribute a certain value to each good (or service) that is sold or purchased. In contemporary societies, where the use of currency is common, such value is generally expressed by a price, in monetary terms. The price a person is willing to pay in exchange for a certain good represents exactly the subjective value that that person attributes to the good. Price increases if the good is more demanded, because of the law of supply and demand: for instance, knowing that someone else might purchase that good (that is relatively scarce, as any other "good" on Earth is scarce, by definition), people are willing to pay more to purchase it first. Then prices are set in a market economy such that they correspond to the values attributed by who wants to buy and sell the good. If the seller fix too high prices and no one buys the good, it means that the good has a greater value for the current owner than for possible purchasers, or alternatively, the owner expects the good is evaluated more in the future. In any case, prices correspond to a precise information: how much people are willing to give, or receive, in exchange for a given asset. The resulting distribution is therefore "patterned" in accordance with the perceived value of a person's actions and services to others. Nothing in this discussion departs from the three principles of justice of the entitlement theory. At the same time, we can observe that Hayek's pattern of distribution "from each as they choose, to each as they are chosen" is analogous to Dworkin's conception of resources valued in terms of what persons' decisions cost others (§2.7). Dworkin himself admit that "both Nozick's theory and equality of resources [...] give a prominent place to the idea of a market, and recommend the distribution that is achieved by a market suitably defined and constrained" [111, 2000]. The difference is that both Hayek and Dworkin admit important exceptions to laissez-faire, unlike Nozick's libertarian position in *Anarchy, State and Utopia*, in which property "necessarily includes absolute control without limits" (Dworkin [88, 2000]). In fact Nozick falters in claiming that such right to property should be absolute, as will be explained in next paragraph. However, he is right in highlighting the issues related to the achievement of patterned distributions – which in some cases may be good reasons why we shouldn't aim at those patterns.

In a free market economy, patterned principles may introduce redistributions or regulations (aimed at pursuing the pattern) which alter the prices of the assets. According to Nozick (and Hayek), when prices (and thus information) are distorted, we are not only giving up economic efficiency, but also the pattern itself is hardly achievable. To grasp this point we might think of the following example. Suppose the government aims at achieving the distributive moral pattern "to each according to her merits". Further assume that the parliament decides high school teachers have greater merits than what calculated before, because – for instance – to become teachers requires big efforts, hard work, or concern for important social values as education. As a consequence, government increases teacher wages. In order to pay teachers, the treasury is forced to make money imposing more taxes, or alternatively printing money, which creates inflation. Some strata of the population may be worst hit by inflation and high prices, including many who don't deserve at all to pay an additional tax or an inflation tax in order to provide higher wages to teachers. In this case, we might say that the State, operating in order to pursue the pattern (to each according to merits), may actually end up contradicting the pattern itself, because indirect and in some cases unpredictable spillover effects of the policies adopted. According to Hayek, pursuing some kind of patterns is only possible in small groups of individuals, such as a family, not in what he calls the "Great Society", that presents far more complex and interdependent mechanisms[88]. In the distribution of costs and benefits that daily occurs in the relations within a family, to achieve a distribution according to merits or equality is relatively simple, while this goal is absolutely out of reach in a complex society, where a central authority has no adequate means of information at its disposal. Within the Great Society different and distant people are unlikely to properly coordinate while pursuing the pattern. It is difficult for every citizen (or a central planner) to get enough information on the various and interdependent activities in

---

[88] See for example Hayek's *Law, Legislation and Liberty*:
> "*The conception through which the atavistic craving for visible common purposes which so well served the needs of the small group today chiefly expresses itself is that of "social justice". It is incompatible with the principles on which the Great Society rests and indeed the opposite of those forces making for its coherence which can truly be called "social". Our innate instincts are here in conflict with the rules of reason we have learned, a conflict we can resolve only by limiting coercion to what is required by abstract rules and by abstaining from enforcing what can be justified only by the desire of particular results*"
>
> Friedrich von Hayek [1982, 307]

society, so as to know which one upsets and which one properly comply with the pattern.

This position resembles Richard Epstein's discussion of hard and easy cases in *Simple Rules for a Complex World* (1995). He states that economists and politicians should concentrate on getting the "easy cases" right but there are, in practice, many areas where governments continue to get "easy cases" wrong, especially in labour market regulation. This is also due to the fact that too much energy is spent in the "hard cases", which involve a great deal of effort, and still have a high failure rate. An example is the decision to build a new airport: enormous costs are involved, and there are consequences for many aspects of life for noise, pollution, traffic, land values, business growth and the like. Such is the complexity of the decision that it is easy to be wrong, even with the best will and ability in the world. Normally those kind of decisions shouldn't be taken by public authorities (in contrast with what Dworkin proposed in *Hard Cases* [1975] and *A Matter of Principles* [1985]). Epstein provides an explanation of how much complex a hard case could be:

> *"if the law seeks to determine a very complicated issue such as the optimum duration of a patent, it is easy to identify an infinite set of permutations. The question of patent duration cannot be effectively decided in isolation, without reference to patent scope, itself a highly technical area. To make matters worse, the field of patentable inventions might be too broad for a general solution to the problem. The answer that seems to work well for pharmaceutical patents may not be as sensible for software. But the moment we decide that different patents classes should have different lengths, someone will be faced with the unhappy task of classifying a new generation of inventions that regrettably straddles a pre-existing set of categories established in ignorance of the future path of technical development: such is the case with computer software, for example"*

Ricard Epstein [2003, 20-21]

According to Buchanan, there is no guarantee a State will get hard cases right. Whether interventions are justified depends on whether government officials are motivated by self-interest as well as a sense of public duty. Weighing up the pros and cons of policy choices requires an unsentimental view of government actions, a position he called "politics without romance" (Buchanan [1999, 45]). Since some will use the political process to obtain favors or privileges at the expense of others, Buchanan argued for a constitutional generality principle to constrain ordinary political decision-making.

Some libertarians think of libertarianism as a position of humility towards the others[89], since they recognize there are hard cases a central planner cannot solve. This position is sharable, but it could hide a trap libertarians have to pay attention to. In fact they can coherently claim to be humble in supporting laissez-faire because they acknowledge *they cannot* know how to improve the situation, but they cannot coherently claim to be humble in supporting laissez-faire because according to them *it is not possible* to know how to improve the situation.

Nozick explains that "no end-state principle or distributional patterned principle of justice can be continuously realized without continuous interference with people's lives" [1974, 164]. In fact any distributional pattern is unstable because overturnable by the voluntary actions of individual persons over time. If people are free to act creating, exchanging, or donating goods, inevitably their "liberty upsets patterns" [160]. Then to maintain the pattern means to "either continually interfere to stop people from transferring resources as they wish to, or continually (or periodically) interfere to take from some persons resources that others for some reason chose to transfer to them"

---

[89] Milton Friedman discussed the topic of humility as one of the basic libertarian beliefs and values: "I have no right to coerce someone else because I cannot be sure that I'm right and he is wrong" (International Society for Individual Liberty's 5th World Libertarian Conference, August 14, 1990).

[163]. It might be said that all persons could voluntarily choose to refrain from actions which would upset the pattern. But against this argument Nozick replies that:

> *"This presupposes unrealistically (1) that all will most want to maintain the pattern (are those who don't, to be "reeducated" or forced to undergo "self-criticism"?), (2) that each can gather enough information about his own actions and the ongoing activities of others to discover which of his actions will upset the pattern, and (3) that diverse and far-flung persons can coordinate their actions to dovetail into the pattern. Compare the manner in which the market is neutral among persons' desires, as it reflects and transmits widely scattered information via prices, and coordinates persons' activities"*
>
> Robert Nozick [1974, 163-164]

In conclusion, Nozick's historical principles of justice match with the ideal of laissez-faire capitalist system: entitlement theory does not allow the existence of authorities with the power to limit the liberty or will of citizens, to the extent that they do not actively harm someone else's properties.

4.3   Libertarianism without Foundation

In the article *Libertarianism without Foundation* (1975), Thomas Nagel explains why Nozick's entitlement theory has no moral justification. The best and most coherent defense of free market economy and individual liberties is to be found in political liberalism, rather than libertarianism. Nozick starts from the unargued premise that individuals have certain inviolable rights (to self-ownership and property), which cannot be intentionally transgressed by other individuals or the State for any purpose. This sort of jusnaturalism, on which libertarianism rely, cannot be a valid justification of a theory of justice in contemporary societies. The existence of a natural law, such as the absolute entitlement to our bodies and the products of our labor, isn't shared by all, yet it could be a minority position considering the relativistic context in which we live. After Hume, Kant, Nietzsche, the death of metaphysics, the raise of scepticism, experimentation and nihilism, the claim to base a political theory on natural laws appears to be merely a naïve attempt comparable to the establishment of a new theology. According to entitlement theory, there are no rights to prevent something bad happens to you, rather only duty of others to not do something bad against you: "it is of the first importance that your right not to be assaulted is *not* a right that everyone do what is required to ensure that you are not assaulted. This cannot be explained simply by the fact that it is bad to be assaulted" (Nagel [1975, 198]). There are no values like "you shouldn't be assaulted", rather only rules like "you shouldn't assault". Therefore Nozick's entitlement theory excludes categorically any consequentialist consideration, endorsing a purely deontological morality. Morality instead should include considerations of both types (§1.7). Nagel puts it in this way (making direct reference to Nozick [1974, 29]):

> *"As Nozick points out, the constraints on action represented by rights cannot be equivalent to an assignment of large disvalue to their violation, for that would make it permissible to violate such a right if by doing so one could prevent more numerous or more serious violations of the same right by others, This is not in general true [...] There is no reason to think that either in personal life or in society the force of every right will be absolute or nearly absolute, i.e., never capable of being overridden by consequential considerations"*
> Thomas Nagel [1975, 199]

Suppose one day manna falls from heaven and accumulated at the center of the main square of the city. It is a divine gift, no one produced it. To distribute manna to the poorest and the most needy doesn't imply any violations of property right or contract related to property exchange. When no violations of rights is at issue, in distributing benefits (or harms) among persons we may achieve certain distributions that are morally perceived as better than others. For example, to distribute manna towards starving people is morally considered better than consuming it among the richest people of the city (at least, it is so for the most of the people living in western democracies). Indeed, we should recognize there are worthwhile ends, like the compensation of inequalities, or the fact of taking care of the needy. Nozick's rights limit the pursuit of worthwhile ends, but there are no reasons why they shouldn't be sometimes overridden if the ends are sufficiently important. Some ends may have priority (for consequentialist reasons) on the pure deontology of Nozick's historical principles of justice, as it may happen in the hypothetical situations the following examples figure out.

The first example regards an old man who built a house on the hill. Over the years, at the foot of the hill a town rises up. At a certain point, thanks to new detection technologies, residents discover the town is at serious flooding risks, unless they build a dyke in the precise site where there is old man's house. Despite town's citizens offer him a generous compensation, including a new bigger house in a similar place, he refuses to leave, arguing he wants to die in the house he built and to which he is attached. If the town was composed of only few families, someone might say they should evacuate, leaving alone the old man. But what if in the town lived 10, 100 or 1000 families? We quite understand that the old man would be deprived of the right to ownership of his house, and that the reasons for this choice are considered moral, despite what Nozick may assert. What libertarians ignore is that without the existence of public authorities, probably town's citizens will "fend for themselves": they will evict the old man by force. The paradox is that without a State safeguarding the old man's property, his property cannot be successfully preserved, since we can easily imagine that town's citizens wouldn't care of his property rights or any presumed "natural law" establishing his ownership. At the same time, if a State was established, why should citizens include in the constitution a purely deontological rule in which only a small group of libertarian citizens believe? In the end, neither with nor without the existence of a State libertarians can successfully claim the entitlement theory be implemented. Public institutions must be founded on a more shared or sharable principle, like equal respect. Self-ownership is an important principle of justice, but it has to be weighted within a framework composed of many other values, including utility, equality or merits. If the State has to be neutral – as far as possible – towards citizens' conception of the good life (as libertarians presumably believe), why it should endorse the very controversial conception of Nozick's entitlement?

Getting back to the example, some libertarians may agree that the old man should be evicted, but only because the lives or properties of other people are at risk. They might say that the right to secure people's lives (which may be derivative of the right of self-ownership), is prior over the right of property. Also the fact of securing the properties of many people may have priority over the right of property of only one person. Indeed, even if libertarians might think that the right of property has no priority over certain principles (like the security of life) they would probably deny that property could be threatened by other kind of interests, like the achievement of welfare or utility: for instance we cannot force people to leave their home in order to build a street. Nonetheless, for certain consequentialist reasons we might consider evictions (when compensated) as morally justifiable even when its purpose is welfare maximisation. Suppose now old man's house lies exactly where the government intends to build a highway, which necessarily crosses that area, because of geography. The highway will be the only connection between two States, and we know with certainty[90] that the construction will involve thousands of families, thousands of workers will get a job and no more starve, the direct and indirect economic effects of new trades will enrich millions of people[91]. Provided these assumptions, purely deontological rules about property right would seem inadequate to meet the sense of justice of most of us.

Another example of different kind may be provided. Suppose an inventor created a device that is a source of energy at very low costs. The invention is clearly original acquisition, then the inventor has the right to patent the device and get the derived earnings. In order to stimulate inventors to conceive new technologies, there are principles promoting scientific progress and economic efficiency which establish that inventors must be able to fully enjoy every possible earning derived from their inventions (also for this reason patent exists). But suppose the inventor dies and the patent is transferred to his son. According to the entitlement theory, the new owner can dispose of the device the way he wants: for instance he may allow to use the device only very few people who can afford to pay a very high price. Suppose this device could solve most of the energy

---

[90] Libertarians often highlight that we cannot have such certainties. In this case divergence from left liberals is about an empirical claim, that is, we cannot resolve a particular hard case. The issue at stake here is not about the possibility to know with certainty the consequences of some policies or actions, rather to test a person's deontological convictions. If a person does not endorse a deontological morality under very narrowly defined assumptions, then she is likely to do the same, to a certain extent, when those assumptions are less restrictive.

[91] Libertarians would object that the highway has to be funded by taxation and citizens might not agree to pay taxes for this purpose. Then assume, for simplicity, that all citizens agree to pay the highway, (apart from the evicted one, indeed), because they are supposed to be certain about the economic consequences of the new highway. Though this assumption is very unlikely to be met in real situations, in this example we have to focus on the problem of eviction, other circumstances are irrelevant.

problems of the world, if used in the proper way. It was the inventor, not his son, to create the new device, the son has no merit at all. Nonetheless, if he wanted he could even legitimately destroy the device, according to the entitlement theory. Is he really entitled to do whatever he wants with the device? Really should the property right be independent from any other moral principle regarding merits, equity, efficiency, or any moral, social or economic circumstance?

Let's see one last example: suppose the parliament introduce the right to own a gun, with libertarians voting in favour. Next year firearm-related death rate increases of 30%. Suppose there seem to be no other explanation to this increase alternative to the introduction of the gun law. For example, no exceptional bloody shootout between gangsters occurred which could have happened even before the introduction of the gun law. Statistics seem clear and there is no bias correlation between the death rate increase and the introduction of the law. Shouldn't libertarians feel in some way responsible for those deaths?[92]

It doesn't matter if the above mentioned examples represent extreme situations very unlikely to happen in reality. If we believe that in those hypothetical situations a purely deontological morality falters, then we are likely to admit the same for more ordinary cases. How distant our moral judgement is placed from a purely deontological conception depends on the sensibility of each one. Contrary to libertarian, liberals don't endorse in an extremist way a purely deontological principle, but tend to reasonably consider morality weighing different principles and social circumstances. So the property right becomes, at least in part, relative, exactly like all the other values. In conclusion, we might say that libertarianism is monistic, deontological and anti-consequentialist, while liberalism is

---

[92] I personally presented all the above mentioned examples to some libertarians. They sided in favour of Nozick's entitlement without any hesitation.

pluralistic and represents a balance between deontology and consequentialism. Political liberalism recognizes the centrality of property rights and tries to preserve them from State interference, but property isn't an absolute, nor it represents the moral foundation of liberalism and liberty. In the western world property has never been that absolute inalienable right to which Nozick refers. As Nagel explains, the right of property "would confer the kind of qualified entitlement that exists in a system under which taxes and other conditions are arranged to preserve certain features of the distribution, while permitting choice, use, and exchange of property compatible with it. What someone holds under such a system will not be *his property* in the unqualified sense of Nozick's system of entitlement" [1975, 201]. In other words, the right of property exists and was shaped in a patterned system, which has always been compatible with taxation or other conditions aimed at preserving determined patterns. In conclusion, the "system", the whole social environment, including public authorities and their coercive monopoly power, pre-existed the property rights, or at least were formed in parallel. Individual rights existed before the *Rechtsstaat* (State of Law)? And does it make sense to speak of *Rechtsstaat* before the formation of the modern State, before the French Revolution, before Magna Charta Libertatum and all the historical processes that have contributed to create it? If it did not exist the State, which was shaped, perhaps, just in a process that tended to the realization of certain patterns, we wouldn't have now individual rights as we know them. So it does not even make sense to think of rights completely independent from "patterns" and prior to them. We cannot disregard thousands of years of history, processes which involved billions of people and complicated political and economic institutions (cf Nagel [1976, 195]).

4.4   Libertarians or Classical Liberals?

Liberals start from the premise that to justify individual rights we cannot rely on natural or unargued laws like self-ownership. Individual rights are not self-evident or self-justified, and contractualism is the only way citizens can agree on the political conception of justice and on the public notion of liberty. Nonetheless, equal respect isn't a principle on which citizens agree ex-post, while stipulating the contract, but is given ex-ante, as a pre-condition of the contract: it explains *why* we should stipulate a contract. The claim is that equal respect is almost universally shared in modern western societies, but it still remains a "non-falsified hypothesis" (recalling Popper's terminology [1959]) since – as Larmore explains – it may happen that modern experience is to dissolve in the light of a new irresistible, all-encompassing Good (see §2.5). Instead, libertarian self-ownership seems to be considered by its promoters as a truth we shall embrace as absolute. Even early liberals who believed in the natural law (instead of a positive law resulting from the contract), recognized limits to property rights. For instance, according to Locke, one has a right to as much as she could use, it's not permissible to have things that are not consumed and will decay and perish. Moreover, there is what Nozick calls "Lockean proviso": the proviso maintains that appropriation of unowned resources is a diminution of the rights of others to it, and would be acceptable only so long as it does not make anyone worse off than they would have been before: "at least where there is enough, and as good, left in common for others" (see Locke [1689 b, V, 33]). Actually, there are just very few authors often considered as adherent of the libertarian front who firmly believed in purely deontological morality and in a completely uncontrolled laissez-faire economic system. Among them, the "first" Nozick (he later disavowed his libertarian theory) and Rothbard. In fact Hayek – just to mention a very influential thinker in the libertarian thought – actually belongs without any doubt to the family of classical liberals. His justification of deontological rules relies on a more sophisticated approach with respect to Nozick's entitlement:

> *"The rules of morals are instrumental in the sense that they assist mainly in the achievement of other human values; however, since we only rarely can know what depends on their being followed in the particular instance, to observe them must be regarded as a value in itself, a sort of intermediate end which we must pursue without questioning its justification in the particular case"*
> Friedrich Von Hayek [1960, 67]

Moreover, as McCann underlines [2002, 22], in Hayek we see also the justification of an apparatus of a social institutions engaged in the promotion of a community or communal interests: "Wherever communal action can mitigate disasters against which the individual can neither attempt to guard himself nor make provision for the consequences, such communal action should undoubtedly be taken" (Hayek [1944, 134]). Therefore Hayek's conception would be more broadly conceived than is typically acknowledged, for the concept of right, the guarantee of which is seen as the defining characteristic of the liberal polity, is itself a common good. Certainly Hayek is willing to concede a place for State action. In general terms, he acknowledges a government role in activities designed "to provide a favorable framework for individual decisions," such as would "supply means which individuals can use for their own purposes", as well as actions dedicated to "the enforcement of the general rules of law" (Hayek [1960, 223]).

Hayekian individualism is "primarily a *theory* of society, an attempt to understand the forces which determine the social life of man" (Hayek [1948, 6]). More importantly, it is a theory of social order predicated on an understanding of men as socially constituted: our "whole nature and character" derives from our social existence [1948, 6]. Its fulfillment requires "the universal acceptance of general principles as the means to create order in social affairs" [1948, 19], its essence being "respect for the individual man *qua* man" (Hayek [1944, 17]). Hayek's individualism thus stands in stark contrast to atomistic approaches which isolate man from society, approaches which provide "no cohesion other than the coercive rules imposed by the state," such that "all social ties [are merely] prescriptive" (Hayek [1948, 23]) [93]. In conclusion, authors like McCann [2002] and Andrew Lister [2011] agree on that Hayek's social philosophy has been widely misrepresented among liberal, libertarian and communitarian thinkers:

> *"At the heart of Friedrich A. Hayek's social philosophy is a regard for the socially-constituted nature of man: the individual is not taken to be asocial or pre-social, but rather it is recognized that society defines the individual. The neglect of this aspect of Hayek's work by both liberal and communitarian, as well as libertarian, writers within political philosophy has led to his position being misrepresented, for Hayek's brand of liberalism is more akin to one variant of modern communitarianism than it is to the libertarian strain of liberal thought"*
> McCann [2002, 5]

Hayek also approved tax imposition and the institution of a "minimum income for everyone": "a sort of floor below which nobody need fall even when he is unable to provide for himself, appears not only to be wholly legitimate protection against a risk common to all, but a necessary part of the Great Society" [1960, 57]. But it is not motivated by the pursuit of a "*just* distribution of incomes" [55] regarding, for instance, merits or equality. Instead, it is motivated by the value that libertarians prize above all others – freedom. Hayek saw the protection of individual liberty as one of the most basic and important political ideals, since freedom is conceived as "that condition of men in which

---

[93] Cf McCann [2002, 14].

coercion of some by others is reduced as much as is possible in society" [57]. But it is not necessarily intended as *negative* liberty: "Though in some of the other senses it may be legitimate to speak of different kinds of freedom, "freedoms from" and "freedoms to", in our sense "freedom" is one, varying in degree but not in kind" [60]. While a concern for freedom in this sense lends strong support to a system of free markets and private property, as well as to skepticism of invasive government, it can also lead to worries about certain forms of coercion within the market. Even if market competition is often a good check against private dominance, there is no good economic reason to believe that it will always be sufficient.

If we understand freedom from arbitrary coercion also in a *positive* way (as "liberty to" rather than just "liberty from"), then we see how the pursuit of freedom and equal opportunity are compatible and complementary. Equal respect and rational dialogue require we are equally free to choose the life we desire, according to our conception of the good. This is a concept of equality demanding that we are "equally constrained" by only the costs our deliberate choices entail for others: "The cost to someone of what he consumes, by way of goods and leisure, and the value of what he adds, through his productive labor or decisions, is fixed by the amount his use of some resource costs others, or his contributions benefit them, in each case measured by their willingness to pay for it" (Dworkin [1985, 207]). Any other interference to this "liberty of choice" is non-neutral towards the conceptions of the good, and interferences (as well as coercion) may occur also within free market mechanisms. Therefore institutions, in order to ensure liberty from those interferences may be also required to actively intervene adjusting market mechanisms. In the real world, coercion can only be minimized, not eliminated, and the coercion of some individuals by others can often be held in check only by the use of coercion itself: "The task of a policy of freedom must therefore be to minimize coercion or its harmful effects, even if it cannot eliminate it completely" (Hayek [1960, 59]). Of course, a basic income needs to be funded by taxation and so would seem to involve the imposition its own kind of coercion. But not for this reason we should believe that all taxation is incompatible with freedom. What makes the coercion of the slavemaster, or the monopolist, so worrisome for Hayek is that it involves the arbitrary imposition of one person's will on another. By contrast, a tax system that is clearly and publicly defined in advance, that imposes only reasonable rates for genuinely public purposes, that is imposed equally upon all, and that is constrained by democratic procedures and the rule of law, might still be constitute interference, but not arbitrary interference[94]. In this regard, Epstein declares that the stereotypical and purely deontological libertarian position is even "ridicule", for this reason he prefers to consider himself a classical liberal:

> *"If the libertarian holds fast to the assumption that all forms of state coercion are equal, then he strips himself of the tools that might allow him to segregate out those state projects that are worth doing and those which are not. Likewise, the rejection of all systems of taxation makes it impossible to distinguish between better and worse systems of taxation and exposes a serious political theory to the most dangerous of refutations – ridicule"*
> Richard Epstein [2003, 31-32]

Epstein recognizes that libertarian should be "not somebody who believes that we are all dewy-eyed individuals who will always work for the best interests of other people. Rather, he recognizes that self-interest is a force that sometimes can be turned to bad ends and sometimes to good ends [2003, 28].

As Hayek, many libertarians favoured, or at least accepted, a minimum income scheme, like Charles Murray [2006] in his

---

[94] See also Matt Zwolinski's article:
http://www.libertarianism.org/columns/why-did-hayek-support-basic-income

book *In Our Hands: A Plan To Replace The Welfare State*. Milton Friedman [1962] preferred to have no income tax at all, but said he did not think it was politically feasible to eliminate it, so in *Capitalism and Freedom* suggested a "less harmful" tax scheme, developing the idea of a progressive "negative income scheme"[95] (which also Dworkin [1985, 208] might acknowledge as a "more efficient and fairer" scheme, than other "targeted programs" of welfare state aiming at particular opportunity of resources).

John Tomasi [2012, V] provides a long list of liberals and libertarians who actually are not blind supporter of laissez-faire. Tomasi does not call attention to these authors (whose passages are partly reported below) in the hope of convincing people on the left of the hidden humanitarian agenda of the political right, rather his aim is "to encourage classical liberals and libertarians to reflect upon the pervasiveness of these expressions of concern about distributive outcomes on the part of philosophers (and, perhaps, politicians) whose work they admire".

Ludwig von Mises complained that advocates of the New Liberalism (social or progressive liberals) "arrogate to themselves the exclusive right to call their own program the program of welfare". Von Mises calls this "a cheap logical trick". Just because classical liberals do not rely upon direct, state-based programs and agencies to secure the material well-being of citizens, this does not mean that classical liberals are any less concerned for the poor (Mises [1998, 830]). Von Mises emphasizes that humans must always cooperate within the framework of societal bonds: "Social man as differentiated from autarkic man must necessarily modify his original biological indifference to the well-being of people beyond his own family. He must adjust his conduct to the requirements of social

---

[95] It consists in a progressive income tax system where people earning below a certain amount receive supplemental pay from the government instead of paying taxes to the government.

cooperation and look upon his fellow men's success as an indispensable condition of his own" (Mises [1985, 14]). In commercial society, no person is an isolated atom, commercial competition is merely one form of social cooperation.

Ayn Rand famously defends a doctrine of egoism and rejects all ideas of distributive justice. Nonetheless, she seems to assert in several passages that capitalism is the system maximizing the welfare of the poor people. After all, even Howard Roark, in the famous speech in his own defense (from Rand's novel *Fountainhead* [1943]) states: "Those who were concerned with the poor had to come to me, who have never been concerned, in order to help the poor".

Geoffrey Brennan [2013] underlines the affinity between Buchanan and Rawls. Like Rawls, Buchanan is a constructivist: the principles of justice are not chosen because they are independently ascertained to be authoritative but rather are authoritative because they are chosen (under a suitably defined set of background conditions that guarantee fairness).

> "*Buchanan always recognized the affinity between his approach and that of John Rawls, and often remarked that his project and Rawls's are very similar, even though 'they have been interpreted differently.' On one notable occasion at a Liberty Fund conference, Anthony Flew was mounting an all-out attack on Rawls's "procrustean" scheme and was astounded at the severity of Buchanan's response. Buchanan was as defensive of Rawls as he was enraged by John F. Kennedy (though the Kennedy issue is another story*"
>
> Geoffrey Brennan [2013, 52, n12]

Actually, as also John Tomasi highlights [2012, V], Mises, Hayek, Buchanan, Rand, Epstein and many other laissez-faire supporters seem to believe that a free market capitalist system would work to the benefit of the least well-off members of society. If it was true, the principle of difference would represent a conception of distributive justice far less distant from a typical libertarian perspective. Of course, this is an empirical claim: it might turn out to be true; it might turn out to be false. Whatever truth value one assigns to this claim, it cannot be denied that it is central for many libertarian authors (they would change their mind if persuaded otherwise?). Jason Brennan [2007, 287-299] seems convinced that an "enthusiastically capitalist society" would do better for the poor than other systems. He suggests a thought experiment (see *Figure 4*), comparing two imaginary societies: the "ParetoSuperiorLand" (a laissez-faire capitalist system) and "FairnessLand" (a property-owning democracy). The initial income distribution is in favour of the poor in FairnessLand, but over time, the relative position of the least well-off of classes in the two societies is reversed.

Figure 4: Brennan's Thought Experiment

	ParetoSuperiorLand			FairnessLand		
	Poor	Middle	Rich	Poor	Middle	Rich
2000	10	20	40	15	19	24
2001	10.4	20.8	41.6	15.3	19.4	24.5
2002	10.8	21.6	43.2	15.6	19.8	25.0
2025	26.7	53.3	106.6	24.6	31.2	39.4
2050	71.1	142.1	284.3	40.4	51.2	64.6
2100	505.1	1010.1	2020.2	108.7	137.7	173.9

It is highly controversial indeed, but what is striking is that if we "suspend the judgement" about this empirical claim, then the positions of authors like Rawls and Hayek become so close that it could be even hard to distinguish between them. Hayek himself was aware of this fact:

> *"the recognition that in such combinations as 'social', 'economic', 'distributive' or 'retributive' justice the term 'justice' is wholly empty should not lead us to throw the baby out with the bath water [...T]here unquestionably [...] exists a genuine problem of justice in connection with the deliberate design of political institutions, the problem to which Professor John Rawls has recently devoted an important book. The fact which I regret and regard as confusing is*

> *merely that in this connection he employs the term 'social justice'"*
> Friedrich Von Hayek [1982, 100]

In *Law, Legislation and Liberty* Hayek states that he decided not to include an extended discussion of Rawls' theory because, "Though the first impression of readers may be different", the differences between his general conception of liberal justice and that of Rawls are "more verbal than substantive". Hayek states that he and Rawls "agree on what is to me the essential point" (Hayek [1982, XIII]). Moreover, he offers a method for assessing social institutions that is strikingly Rawlsian: uncertainty about social position combined with some uncertainty about genetic potential and about specific tastes and interests closely resembles Rawls' veil of ignorance (cf Lister [2011]).

> *"we should regard as the most desirable order of society one which we would choose if we knew that our initial position in it would be decided purely by chance (such as the fact of being born into a particular society). Since the attraction such chance would possess for any particular adult individual would probably be dependent on the particular skills, capacities and tastes he has already acquired, a better way of putting this would be to say that the best society would be that in which we would prefer to place our children if we knew that their position in it would be determined by lot"*
> Friedrich Von Hayek [1982, 132]

To maximize the chances of each individual picked up randomly is really different from what is required by the difference principle? Hayek thinks his proposal of liberal system best improves the chances of all citizens, included the poorest, to achieve their purposes and mutually provide their respective needs: "The most important of the public goods for which government is required is thus not the direct satisfaction of any particular needs, but the securing of conditions in which the individuals and smaller groups will have favourable opportunities of mutually providing for their respective needs" (Hayek [1982,

170]). Of the greatest importance for the individual is not the freedom to act indiscriminately, in selfish pursuit of her own well-being, but rather the "freedom some person may need in order to do things beneficial to society. This freedom we can assure to the unknown person only by giving it to all" (Hayek [1960, 32]).

In light of these unexpected (at first glance) statements, Hayek could be accused of contradicting himself. Actually Hayek focuses on what he sees as the pernicious tendencies of talk about "social justice" at the level of public policy. In the context of the political debates of his days, he notes that appeals to social justice are enormously effective: "Almost every claim for government action on behalf of particular groups is advanced in its name, and if it can be made to appear that a certain measure is demanded by 'social justice', opposition to it will rapidly weaken" (Hayek [1982, 229]). When invoked in public debates about whether or not to create some new governmental social service program, Hayek complains that the invocations of social justice have an "open sesame" effect (Hayek [1982, 231]). The more government succeeds in equalizing opportunities, the stronger becomes the demand that remaining handicaps must be removed. This would go on "until government literally controlled every circumstance which could affect any person's well-being". Thus "any attempt" to realize equality of opportunity beyond government provision of services that can be justified on other grounds "is apt to produce a nightmare" (Hayek [1982, 247]). Hayek rejects the value of equal opportunity, at the same time accepting formal equality of opportunity, although he doesn't say that this is a requirement of social justice: "there is also much to be said in favour of government providing on an equal basis the means for the schooling of minors" [247]. He points out that such measures "would still be very far from creating real equality of opportunity" [247], which would require that government "control the whole physical and human environment of all persons" [247]. The obvious response to this claim is that even if 100% equal opportunity would require a totalitarian state, we may attempt to achieve fair equal opportunity up to the point at which it threatens personal liberty, maybe thanks to proper constitutional constraints.

Hayek's basic philosophical and normative assumptions do not by themselves require or even do much to support his conclusions about law and policy. What generates his conclusions is a set of empirical claims. Moreover, he bypasses the problem of assessing the market from the perspective outcomes talking about "desirability" instead of "justice". The real problem is that Hayek has a sort of ideological bias against the idea of social justice, and this is the reason why the debate between left and right has always been likely to grind on a halt. Hayekian rejection of any notion of "social justice", combined with Nozick's purely deontological approach, are the undoing of a worthwhile political debate between left and right. But while Hayek never gave up his condemnation of the idea of "social justice", Nozick in *The Examined Life* (1989) strikingly and unexpectedly criticizes the theory of justice he offered in *Anarchy, State and Utopia*: "The libertarian position I once propounded now seems to me seriously inadequate". In fact there are "things we choose to do together through government in solemn marking of our human solidarity, served by the fact that we do them together in this official fashion" [1989, 287]. He severely underlines that democracy is a fundamental value because the vote is "expression and symbolic affirmation of our status as autonomous and self-governing beings whose considered judgements or even opinions have to be given weight equal to those of others" and "we want expressions of the values that concern us and bind us together". In the following quotation, he also provides what we may consider the best explanation of why democracy and difference principle should be acknowledged as an *original Compact* binding us together, as I tried to suggest in this essay (§3.6-3.7):

> "*We want our individual lives to express our conceptions of reality (and of responsiveness to that); so too we want the institutions demarcating our lives together to express and saliently symbolize our desired mutual relations. Democratic institutions and the liberties coordinate with them are not simply effective means toward controlling the powers of government and directing these toward matters of joint concern; they themselves express and symbolize, in a pointed and official way, our equal human dignity, our autonomy and powers of self-direction [...] Joint political action does not merely symbolically express our ties of concern, it also constitutes a relational tie itself. The relational stance, in the political realms, leads us to want to express and initiate ties of concern to our fellows. And if helping those in need, as compared to further bettering the situation of those already well off, counts as relationally more intense and enduring from our side and from the side of the receivers also, then the relational stance can explain what puzzles utilitarianism, viz., why a concern for bettering others' situation concentrates especially upon the needy. If manna descended from heaven to improve the situation of the needy, all without our aid, we would have to find another way to jointly express and intensify our relational ties*"
>
> Robert Nozick [1989, 286-288]

Conclusions

In the first chapter of this essay I presented the idea of neutrality as abstention – by political institutions – from intervening in individual's private sphere. The State shouldn't incentivize, disincentivize or forbid the pursuit of whatever aim individuals intend to achieve, following their conception of the good life. This idea of neutrality traces the ideas of religious tolerance and secular State which had a central role in western history since XVI century (§1.2). The idea of tolerance extended to other spheres of human life – besides religion – so as to include cultural, ethnic, linguistic and ideological differences: neutrality can be seen as the tolerance of the age of multiculturalism (§1.3). Neutrality towards conceptions of the good life can be achieved making appeal to the universal procedure of rational dialogue (§2.1), but the parties involved in the dispute may not want to follow this procedure without good reason. The motivation leading us to start the rational dialogue is equal respect (§2.2), a moral principle widely accepted in modern western democracies, since it finds its roots in our common history. It doesn't embody a comprehensive liberal conception of the good life, because it doesn't rely on the concept of individual autonomy which classical liberal authors have often endorsed (§2.4). Rather, it might even represent what we consider morality itself (§2.5).

To comply with the requirements of equal respect and rational dialogue, not only the State should abstain from encouraging or discouraging any conception of the good life, but it is also necessary to operate in order to ensure everyone is in the position to pursue her conception of the good life, "equally" to each other. Anyone wishing to make the life of the thief or assassin may rise obstacles to the free choice of others who wish to pursue their conception of life. Our freedom ends where another person's freedom begins, otherwise, to use Rawls' words: "each person is to have an equal right to the most extensive scheme of equal basic liberties compatible with a similar scheme of liberties for others" (first principle of justice). For this reason public institutions must have an active role in imposing certain prohibitions or encouraging or discouraging certain behaviours. To be equally free, it is necessary to put some constraints to liberty, but those constraints shall be equal for all.

In the economic world, the idea of free market helps us to specify the conception of "equal constraints" (§4.1 and §4.4). In fact our life choices imply a cost or a benefit to others, which impacts – directly or indirectly – on their life choices (see §2.7). Our decisions are permitted to the extent that we "afford" them, paying their cost, established by those who have to give up their options to allow ours. Everyone has the same constraint because we cannot have at a certain price what others are not willing to give up at that price. If we desire a particular thing we have to pay the price defined by market interactions, such that the value (price) of one thing cannot be arbitrarily established by one person's conception of the good life. In this way all conceptions of the good life count as equal and all persons are, in this sense, treated equally. Assume we want to purchase a house: we have to pay the cost established by those who have to give up on it, that is, the seller, or another potential buyer who "competes" with us, so concurring to establish the price. If we have more cash on hand to buy the house than others, it means we have paid the cost of other renunciations, for example, we worked or studied more (in order to have a more profitable job), giving up free time or enjoyable activities. Institutions shall not interfere with the voluntary cooperation among individuals so distorting market prices, because it would inevitably favour or put at a disadvantage certain conceptions of the good life. An intervention may encourage or discourage those conceptions prompting people to work or study more, or to get more profitable or unprofitable jobs, or to be an artist rather than an engineer or a hermit.

However, in a free market framework there are disadvantaged people who do not have the same opportunities of each other in choosing the life they desire, because they start with a smaller amount of resources to be used to pursue their ends or desires. The problem is to conceive policies which ensure an equal amount of resources, without unequally hinder individuals' freedom to pursue their conception of the good life. This is not possible, not only in practice but also in theory. Public authority shall not pursue an "egalitarian" distribution of wealth or "product" of social cooperation, since equality of wealth or welfare (§2.6) are not legitimately pursued according to the neutrality towards the conceptions of the good life (otherwise unequal constraints to liberty would be introduced). On the other hand, people cannot be endowed with the same amount of resources at a certain point in time, because it would require a redistribution upsetting all the preceding decisions and life choices of everybody. The solution to the problem of the disadvantaged is represented by an insurance against brutal luck, funded by compulsory taxation[96], plus an inheritance tax, specifically on second or third generation wealth (§4.1). Further measures in favour of equality of opportunity might be established by public authorities (and funded by taxation) according to the demand of the difference principle, understood as it has been exposed in the third chapter. Indeed, among these "measures" there is education, which not only promotes equality of opportunity, but is also necessary so that the moral principles on which the liberal State rely are understood by its citizens, who shall maintain their support to liberal institutions. These

---

[96] Other types of "insurance" funded by compulsory taxation (including security forces, army, health care, etc.) might be justified both through philosophical and economic arguments, but this essay doesn't explore these issues.

measures require not only a minimal State guaranteeing "negative liberty" (as Berlin intended it [1958]), but also a more active intervention, ensuring opportunities to allow us to develop the life we desire, based on our conception of the good. This essay faces the challenge of justifying the pursuit of some "positive liberties" (policies aiming at equal opportunity) from a neutral perspective based on equal respect.

The difference principle may also be justified under a libertarian perspective (§3.5-3.6), provided that some (questionable) empirical claims are accepted (§4.4). It may be that an imaginary society presenting the right level of inheritance tax, and which has adopted all the necessary forms of publicly funded insurance and education, would not need to implement further policies in order to promote equality of opportunity, since the principle of difference would be automatically satisfied. There is no need to upset the free market dynamics, nor a central planner should intervene heavily in citizens' life and economic plans. On the other hand, equality of opportunity (as well as a concern for the needy) is an issue often dear also to thinkers belonging to the libertarian school of thought (or close to it). For this reason Hayek or Buchanan's theories are much closer to Rawls' theory of justice as fairness than what generally expected. The fact remains, however, that purely deontological theories of justice (as expressed in earlier Nozick's writings or Rothbard's ethics of liberty, §4.2), fails to fully recognize the heterogeneous patterns of moral complexities (§4.3, see also §1.7). This is a serious mistake, which Nozick acknowledges in his most recent writings (§4.4).

The paralysis and ineffectiveness of politics towards the most important issues of our day are frequently due to the presence of ideological barriers, which arise not only in the political debate within palace politics, but at all levels of society. Rational dialogue represents the way forward in order to start a fruitful debate with intellectual honesty, and equal respect is its moral justification, namely the reason why we shall resolve disputes in this procedural way. The first part of this essay is devoted to these issues. On the other hand, the second part shows that – for what concerns many of the most important political issues of our day – the parties involved in the dispute are often not so distant as we may expect. This fact represents a further motivation to carry on the debate, putting aside ideological barriers. There are some flaws in libertarian theories that must be overcome, as an excessive attachment to a deontological ethic, or the hostility to the abstract concept of social justice (§4.4), but once moved beyond these prejudices, left and right can find a common ground for a fruitful debate, on whose outcome our future depends.

Appendix

A Critique to Bentham's Utilitarianism

Bentham's postulates are:
a) The only real interests are those of the individuals[97]
b) The interest or utility of the community exists only as the sum of individual interests[98]

First of all, to reach the greatest net balance of utility, maximizing in this way the welfare of the community as a whole, it is not obvious that it is possible to evaluate, for different individuals, utility and dis-utility on the same scale and with the same degree of intensity. Even if it was possible, individual's interests would be necessarily conflicting and wouldn't represent a positive sum game (except in the conditions later analysed). This implies that the outcome of the collective choice conflicts with the principle of individual utility. At this point, it's not clear why the outcome that emerges at the collective level should be more valid and/or "more true" than the one at the individual level. It could be only motivated by the assumption of an "organic" view of society, to be postulated in axiomatic terms together with the second Bentham's postulate. Moreover, it is

---

[97] See *An Introduction to the Principles of Morals and Legislation* (1789):
"*It has been shown that the happiness of the individuals, of whom a community is composed, that is their pleasures and their security, is the end and sole end which the legislator ought to have in view: the sole standard, in conformity to which each individual ought, as far as depends upon the legislator, to be made to fashion his behaviour*"
Jeremy Bentham [1970, 147]

[98] Bentham defines the "community" as "a fictitious body, composed of the individual persons who are considered as constituting as it were its members. The interest of the community then is, what? – the sum of the interests of the several members who compose it" [1970, 126]. By providing security for the interests of the community, the interests of its individual components will automatically be taken into account.

not clear how there could be a "collective judgement" of the entire society, as distinct from the judgement of the individuals. The utility of the community is in fact the sum of individual utilities and derived from them. According to Andrea Villani, in Bentham's theory contradiction occurs not only in relation to the outcome of whatever choice would be made, but also in relation to the two postulates as starting point (Villani [1988, 176-189]).

In order to resolve this problem, we may provide two interpretations of Bentham's theory: 1) utilitarianism leads to a "collective choice" where some individuals are "sacrificed" or 2) each individual, in calculating her own utility function, introduces as a variable the utility (estimated, assumed) of others, so that the final choice will maximize, at the same time, individual and collective utility (positive sum game).

It's not necessarily possible to maximize both individual and collective utility even if individuals were all perfectly rational. We should assume in fact that the utility individuals sacrifice for a greater benefit in the future could be equal or less than the utility they gain in other forms. For example, if one gives up a certain amount of goods (utility, or anyway goods in a broad sense) in favour of others, she should suppose, in a long-term perspective, to gain equal or greater goods produced by other processes, triggered by the increased utility of others, in a virtuous circle benefiting all society and each particular individual at the same time. The mechanism might also be conceived in this way: if one gives up a certain amount of utility/goods she should for certainty get equal or greater utility derived from the happiness of those benefiting of the additional goods now at their disposal, since they could become more willing to help her, or less violent; or again, their pleasure might bring happiness to her, supposing each individual enjoys the increased utility of others, thanks to her altruistic and empathetic character, which easily explains the interdependence of her utility and the utility of others. Outside this strong requirement, really hard to be met in reality, even if all individuals were rational we wouldn't maximize social and individual utility at the same time.

In the end, to calculate individual utility including the preferences of other individuals seems to completely upset Bentham's first postulate, in favour of a rational choice made by an ideal, rational and omniscient legislator, assumed to be impartial and sympathetic to all. The ruler would be considered as a God, or an "enlightened tyrant". The "interests" taken into account by the ruler would lose their correspondence with what we normally would have considered as individual interests in daily lives of citizens. Interests would become part of an organic whole, something more abstract and devoid of the subjective specificity of individuals. In this holistic conception of society the ultimate "solution" would emerge without the need for a social dimension, and the ruler would assume arbitrarily what individual preferences consist in.

Bibliography

Ackerman B.A. (1980), *Social Justice in the Liberal State*, New Haven: Yale University Press

Arendt H. (1968), *Eichmann in Jerusalem: A Report on the Banality of Evil*, New York: Viking Press

Arrow K. (1951), *Social Choice and Individual Values*, New York: Wiley

Barry B. (1995), *Justice as Impartiality*, Oxford: Oxford University Press

Bayle P. (2000), *Various Thoughts on the Occasion of a Comet* (1682), New York: State University of New York Press

Bembo P., Boccacccio G., Giuntini F., Ridolfi L. A. (1555), *Il Decamerone di M. Giovanni Boccaccio, nuouamente stampato, con vn raccoglimento di tutte le sentense, in questa sua opera da lui vsate. Aggiunteci le annotationi di tutti quei luoghi, che di queste cento nouelle, da monsig. Bembo, per ossurustione & intelligenza della thoscana lingua, sono stati nelle sue Prosa allegati*, Lyon: Guglielmo Rouillio (Bibliothèque du Palais des Arts, Lille)

Bentham J. (1970), *An Introduction to the Principles of Morals and Legislation* (1789), London: Athlone

Berlin I. (1968), *Two Concepts of Liberty* in Berlin's *Four Essays on Liberty*, Oxford: Oxford University Press

– (1990), *The Crooked Timber of Humanity: Chapters in the History of Ideas*, London: John Murray

Brennan G. (2013), *Liberty Matters: James Buchanan: An Assessment*, in The Collected Liberty Matters n.1-10, Indianapolis: Liberty Fund

Brennan J. (2007), *Rawls' Paradox*, Constitutional Political Economy 18, n. 4

Buchanan J. (1999), *Logical Foundations of Constitutional Liberty*, Indianapolis: Liberty Fund

Buchanan J, Lomasky L. (1984), *The Matrix of Contractarian Justice*, Social Philosophy and Policy 2, pp. 12-32

Castiglioni L., Mariotti S. (2007), *IL – Vocabolario della Lingua Latina* (1966), Torino: Loescher

Cohen G.A. (2008), *Rescuing Justice & Equality*, Cambridge (MA): Harvard University Press

De Jasay A. (1991), *Choice, Contract, Consent. A restatatement of liberalism*, London: Institute of Economic Affairs

De Werbocz S. et al. (1779), *Corpus Juris Hungarici*, Buda: Typis Regiae Universitatis

Del Bò C. (2011), *La neutralità liberale*, APhEx n. 4
– (2014), *La neutralità necessaria. Liberalismo e religione nell'età del pluralismo*, Pisa: Edizioni ETS

Dodaro M. (2011), *La critica comunitarista al liberalismo rawlsiano*, i-lex. n. 13-14

Dworkin R. (1975), *Hard Cases*, Harvard Law Review, Vol 88, n. 6
– (1978), *Liberalism. In Public and Private Morality*, Cambridge (MA): Cambridge University Press
– (1985), *A Matter of Principle*, London: Harvard University Press

– (2000), *Sovereign Virtue: the Theory and Practice of Equality*, London: Harvard University Press

Epstein R. (1985), *Takings: Private Property and the Power of Eminent Domain*, Cambridge (MA): Harvard University Press
– (1995) *Simple Rules for a Complex World*, Cambridge (MA): Harvard University Press
– (2003) *Free Markets Under Seige: Cartels, Politics and Social Welfare*, IEA Occasional Paper n. 132

Ferrara A. (2009), *La forza dell'esempio. Il paradigma del giudizio*, Milano: Feltrinelli

Fichte J.G. (1973), *Schriften zur Revolution* (1793), ed. by B. Willms, Frankfurt-Berlin-Wien: Ullstein

Fishkin J. (1989), *Review of Charles Larmore's Patterns of Moral Complexity*, Political Theory, n. 17 (4)

Friedman M. (1962), *Capitalism and Freedom*, Chicago: University of Chicago Press

Galeotti A.E. (1992), *La tolleranza. Una proposta pluralista*, Napoli: Liguori

Grotius H. (1993), *De Jure Belli ac Pacis* (1625), ed. by B.J.A. De Kanter van Hettinga Tromps, Aalen: Scientia Verlag

Habermas J. (1990), *Moral Consciousness and Communicative Action*, Cambridge (MA): MIT Press

Harsanyi J.C. (1975), *Can the Maximin Principle Serve as a Basis for Morality? A Critique of John Rawls's Theory* in The American Political Science Review 69 (2)
– (1976), *Essays on Ethics, Social Behavior, and Scientific Explanation*, Dordrecht: Reidel

Hart, H.L.A. (1975), *Rawls on Liberty and Its Priority*, in *Reading Rawls. Critical Studies of "A Theory of Justice"*, Oxford: N. Blackwell

Hayek F.A. (1944) *The Road to Serfdom*, Chicago: University of Chicago Press
– (1948), *Individualism and Economic Order*, Chicago: University of Chicago Press
– (1960), *The Constitution of Liberty*, Chicago: University of Chicago Press
– (1982), *Law, Legislation and Liberty*, London: Routledge
– (2009), *Individualism and Economic Order* (1972), Auburne (Alabama): Ludwig Von Mises Institute

Hume D. (1965), *Treatise on Human Nature* (1738), edited by L.A. Selby-Bige, Oxford: Oxford University Press

Georges K.E. (2002), *Georges* (1950) italian version edited by Calonghi F., Torino: Rosenberg & Sellier

Landi M. (2005), *Due idee di tolleranza*, Interdipendenza n.1, pp. 15-16,

Larmore C. (1987), *Patterns of Moral Complexity*, Cambridge (MA): Cambridge University Press
– (1996), *Morals of Modernity*, Cambridge (MA): Cambridge University Press
– (2008), *The Autonomy of Morality*, Cambridge (MA): Cambridge University Press

Latouche S. (2011), *De-growth, Inequality and Poverty*, in Ventura P., Calderon E., Tiboni M., *Sustainable development Policies for Minor Deprived Urban Communities*, Milano: McGraw-Hill pp. 71-79

Lister A. (2011), *The 'Mirage' of Social Justice: Hayek Against (and For) Rawls*, CSSJ Working Papers Series

Locke J. (1689, a), *A Letter Concerning Toleration*, London: Awnsham Churchill
– (1689, b), *Two Treatises of Government*, London: Awnsham Churchill

Lomasky L. (2005), *Libertarianism at Twin Harvard*, Social Philosophy and Policy, Volume 22, n.1

Lottieri C. (2001), *Il pensiero libertario contemporaneo*, Macerata: Liberlibri

MacIntyre A. (1981), *After Virtue*, London: Duckworth

May K.O. (1952), *A Set of Independent Necessary and Sufficient Conditions for Simple Majority Decision* in Econometrica 20, pp. 680-684

Machiavelli N. (2008), *Il Principe* (1532), Milano: Feltrinelli

McCann C.R. (2002), *F.A. Hayek: The Liberal as Communitarian*, The Review of Austrian Economics, 15:1, 5–34

Mill J.S. (1972), *Utilitarianism. On Liberty. Representative Government* (1859), London: Dent

Mises L.V. (1998), *Human Action: A Treatise On Economics* (1949), Auburne (Alabama): Ludwig Von Mises Institute
– (1985), *Liberalism: The Classical Tradition* (1927), New York: The Foundation for Economic Education

Montefiore A. (1975), *Neutrality and Impartiality: The University and Political Commitment*, Cambridge: Cambridge University Press

Murray C. (2006), *In Our Hands: A Plan To Replace The Welfare State*, Washington: Aei Press

Nagel T. (1975) *Libertarianism without Foundations*, The Yale Law Journal, Volume 85, Issue 1, 136-149
– (2006, a), *Progressive But Not Liberal*, The New York Review of Books, Vol. 53, n. 9
– (2006, b), *The Case for Liberalism: An Exchange*, The New York Review of Books, Vol. 53, n. 15

Nicholas of Cusa (2007), *Epistola ad Rodericum Sancium de Arevalo* (1442), Hamburg: Meiner

Nozick R. (1974), *Anarchy, State, and Utopia*, New York, Basic Books
– (1989), *The Examined Life*, New York: Simon & Schuster

Ottonelli. V (2010), *Leggere Rawls*, Bologna: Il Mulino

Pesce M. (2008), *I monoteismi e quello che le donne e gli uomini decidono di farne*, Annali di Storia dell'esegesi n. 25, pp. 105-158

Plattner M.F. (1979), *Welfare State versus Redistributive State* in Public Interest n. 55

Popper K (1959), *The Logic of Scientific Discovery*, London: Routledge

Przeworskim A. (1999), *Minimalist Conception of Democracy: A Defense*, in *Democracy's Value*, eds. Ian Shapiro and Casiano Hacker-Cordòn, Cambridge (UK): Cambridge University Press

Rand A. (1943), *The Fountainhead*, Indianapolis: Bobbs-Merrill

Rawls, J. (1971) *A Theory of Justice*, Cambridge (MA): Harvard University Press, 1971
– (1993), *Political Liberalism*, New York: Columbia University Press
– (1995), *Political Liberalism: Reply to Habermas* in The Journal of Philosophy Vol. 92, n. 3, 132-180
– (1999), *Reply to Alexander and Musgrave*, in *Collected Papers*, ed Samuel Freeman, Cambridge (MA): Harvard University Press

– (2001), *Justice as Fairness: a Restatment*, Cambridge (MA): Harvard University Press

Raz J. (1986), *The Morality of Freedom*, Oxford: Clarendon Press

Reichlin M. (2008), *Sulla fondazione e la validità delle norme morali: tra deontologia e teleologia*, Questioni di Bioetica n. 7

Rothbard M.N. (1973), *For a New Liberty: The Libertarian Manifesto*, Auburn (Alabama): Ludwig Von Mises Institute
– (1998) *The Ethics of Liberty* (1982), New York: New York University Press

Sandel M. J. (1982), *Liberalism and the Limits of Justice*, Cambridge (MA): Cambridge University Press
– (1984), *The Procedural Republic and the Unencumbered Self*, Political Theory, Vol. 12, n. 1, pp. 81-96
– (1989), *Moral Argument and Liberal Toleration: Abortion and Homosexuality*, 77 Cal. L. Rev. 521.
– (2006), *The Case for Liberalism: An Exchange*, The New York Review of Books, Vol. 53, n. 15

Schumpeter J.A. (1950), *Capitalism, Socialism, and Democracy*, New York: Harper and Row

Seglow J. (2003), *Neutrality and Equal Respect: On Charles Larmore's Theory of Political Liberalism*, The Journal of Value Inquiry n. 37, pp. 83-96

Sen A. (1986), *Choice, Welfare, and Measurement*, Cambridge (MA): MIT Press
– (2009), *The Idea of Justice*, Cambridge (MA): Harvard University Press

Thucydides (2007), *La Guerra del Peloponneso (History of the Peloponnesian War)* (431-404 B.C.), Milano: Mondadori

Tomasi J. (2012), *Free Market Fairness*, Princetown: Princeton University Press

Treccani G. (2009), *Enciclopedia Italiana di scienze, lettere ed arti* (1929), Roma: Istituto dell'Enciclopedia Italiana

Tsebelis G (2002), *Veto Players: How Political Institutions Work*, Princeton: Princeton University Press

Veca S (1986), *Utilitarismo e contrattualismo. Un contrasto fra giustizia allocativa e giustizia distributiva* in *Utilitarismo oggi*, eds E. Lecaldano and S. Veca, Roma-Bari: Laterza, pp. 97-141

Verza A. (1998), *Neutralismo Liberale. Il dibattito Anglo-Americano*, Milano: Università degli studi di Milano: tesi di dottorato X ciclo

Villani A. (1988), *Giustizia distributiva e scelte collettive*, Milano: I.S.U. Università Cattolica, 1988

Voltaire (2000), *Treatise on Tolerance* (1763), Cambridge (UK): Cambridge University Press

Waldron, J. (1993), *Liberal Rights*, Cambridge (MA): Cambridge University Press

Walzer M. (1983), *Spheres of Justice: a Defense of Pluralism and Equality*, New York: New York Basic Book
– (1987), *Interpretation and Social Criticism*, Cambridge (MA): Harvard University Press

Weber M. (1994), *Political writings*, Cambridge (UK): Cambridge University Press

Zuckert M. (2002), *Launching Liberalism: On Lockean Political Philosophy*, Lawrence: University Press of Kansas